Purchasing Population Health

Purchasing Population Health

Paying for Results

David A. Kindig, M.D., Ph.D.

Ann Arbor

The University of Michigan Press

Copyright © by the University of Michigan 1997
All rights reserved
Published in the United States of America by
The University of Michigan Press
Manufactured in the United States of America
♾ Printed on acid-free paper
2000   1999   4   3

A CIP catalog record for this book is available from the British Library.

Library of Congress Cataloging-in-Publication Data

Kindig, David A.
    Purchasing population health : paying for results / David A.
  Kindig.
       p.   cm.
    Includes bibliographical references and index.
    ISBN 0-472-10893-X (cloth)
    1. Medical policy—United States—Decision making.   2. Health
planning—United States.   3. Outcome assessment (Medical care)—
United States.   4. Medical care—United States—Cost effectiveness.
I. Title.
RA395.A3K52   1997
338.4′33621′0973—dc21   97-29010
                                                     CIP

To my parents,
for their love and for my value formation

•

To the taxpayers of Wisconsin,
for making my sabbatical possible
through generous support of their
great state university

Foreword

Not since Victor Fuchs's classic *Who Shall Live? Health, Economics, and Social Choice* (1974) was published in 1974 has anyone attempted such a critical analysis of the factors affecting population health and health care in the United States. Drawing on his experience as a clinician, manager of national community health initiatives, manager of major academic health centers, teacher, and policy analyst, David Kindig has given us a lucid, comprehensive analysis with a prescription for action. While Victor Fuchs changed the way many of us thought about health and the limited role of medical care to population health, Kindig has provided us with the means to link measures of health status with health plans, public health agencies, and provider performance in order to improve the health of the population.

Dr. Kindig has the advantage of the twenty years of research on issues related to population health since the release of Fuchs's book, research that has been summarized recently in Evans, Barer, and Marmor's book, *Why Are Some People Healthy and Others Not?* (1994), that he draws on for his basic conceptual model. He also has the advantage of being able to review developments in health economics, management, and health care, particularly the dramatic impact of market forces and managed care during the past decade. In drawing on the evolving ideas as well as the knowledge gained from the current experience of managed care and public health, Kindig has quite effectively accomplished his mission:

> to explore these relationships and put forth a practical approach to change. **Purchasing population health** is a synthesis of medical care, public health, health economics, sociology, and modern management, with the goal of achieving the most health for every precious dollar spent.

Central to this book is Kindig's vision of linking a specific outcome measure of population health, Health Adjusted Life Expectancy (HALE), to investments in medical care, public health, and the nonmedical determinants of health. Unlike many of the measures traditionally used to measure the health of the population, this outcome measure combines both the length and quality of life. While the National Center for Health Statistics/Centers for Disease Control and Prevention/U.S. Public Health Service has spent years developing measures for years of healthy life, it has not linked this to purchasing. Although the idea is compelling, it cannot be accomplished without a significant improvement in the current fragmented data systems in the United States. In their paper, "Making a Powerful Connection: The Health of the Public and the National Information Infrastructure" (Office of the Assistant Secretary for Health, U.S. Dept. of Health and Human Services, Report of US PHS Public Health Data Policy Coordinating Committee, July 6, 1995), Lasker, Humphreys, and Braithwaite identify the elements that will be required to create a logically integrated health information system in which information once collected can serve multiple purposes. To be able to hold both public health agencies, other health agents, and health plans accountable, an integrated health information system is essential. It must be able to provide data, not just at the national level, but at the state, local, and health plan level.

In addition to his major contributions in focusing on economic incentives, population health, performance measurement, and accountability incorporated in his concept of Purchasing Population Health, Kindig has provided an excellent review of the determinants of health, the forces that drive health care costs, the policies designed to affect costs, the concept of diminishing marginal returns, the limits of more and more investments in medical care, rationing, and the needs of different populations. Even without his pioneering effort to develop the concept of Purchasing Population Health, this would be a very valuable book for all those interested in the most important health policy issues as we enter the twenty-first century.

Philip Lee, M.D.
San Francisco, California

Preface

While this book is the concrete product of a sabbatical year of study and reflection in 1995–96, its purpose is not primarily academic. Our health care system is at a critical point regarding costs and quality and is on the cusp of moving toward outcomes based purchasing. The book is primarily intended for an audience of business, political, and professional leaders whose understanding and support for a new health outcome purchasing standard will be critical. If the argument is successful, they will begin to think that more outcomes can be obtained from private and public investments, and they will insist on such outcome performance from provider systems. I also hope that the message will be useful to students of the health professions and health management, and that the references provided will assist those who wish to review much of the original research in some depth.

In addition to the year of intense intellectual activity, the argument set forth draws heavily on the wonderfully broad set of professional experiences I have been privileged to have since beginning my medical and doctoral study at the University of Chicago in 1962. In those seven years, I gained basic medical skills as well as an appreciation for careful empirical methods. It was on Chicago's south side as well that I emerged from a relatively protected personal and collegiate life into a social environment and a time in history that demanded sensitivity and awareness to the pressing issues of the day.

While I have learned from and sometimes envied the freer and more radical passion of friends and colleagues, my natural inclination has always been to spend more time and energy in practical and realistic approaches to changing institutions from within. As president of the Student American Medical Association in 1967–68, I provided leadership for moving that organization toward pragmatic activism for changing medical education and health delivery, such as our role in establishing community health experiences and the National Health Service Corps.

The critical incident in my career was the opportunity offered me by Harold Wise to leave biomedical science in Chicago to establish the Residency Program in Social Medicine at the Martin Luther King Jr.

Neighborhood Health Center and Montefiore Hospital in the Bronx. This was a spectacular opportunity for a newly minted physician and one that set me on my career path as a medical manager of federal governmental programs, a large urban nonprofit hospital, and an academic health science center. The managerial and philosophical origins of the ideas and argument set forth in this book took root there as well. At Martin Luther King, the ideas were imprinted early that health was more than medical care but also involved jobs and environment, that teams of different health professionals were necessary for efficient and culturally sensitive delivery, and that the health of a neighborhood was as dependent on those who did not come in for care as those who did. This broader and more complex understanding was gained very early in my career and in a more fundamental way than was taught in medical school or to those who remained within the hospital/academic setting.

A critical negative lesson was also learned there—that good ideas such as many of those embodied in the Office of Economic Opportunity health programs could not be sustained as demonstration projects, since essential components often are stripped away as time passes and social and political attitudes change. This managerial maturity was greatly enhanced under the demanding tutelage of Martin Cherkasky at Montefiore Hospital and Medical Center. I had never aspired to hospital administration, but the opportunity to work and learn in his unique institution of social commitment and tough management was wonderful and painful at the same time. By the age of 40 I understood what "no margin, no mission" meant and had a clearer view of the difficult balance of using money and power for socially useful outcomes. I also learned that organizations cannot be overly regulated from outside if they are to achieve maximal effectiveness but that some overarching outcome and evaluation mechanism is necessary so that process, inertia, self-interest, and politics do not impede progress toward mission. I learned that an organization's budget of dollars and time is its true statement of purpose, regardless of what the mission statement says. The importance of building desired outcomes into stable and appropriate financial incentives and managerial processes was crystallized in these experiences.

Another critical incident in the idea of purchasing outcomes occurred while I was a commissioner on the Medicare Prospective Payment Assessment Commission in 1991. Hospital rates were moderating under the Diagnostic Related Groups (DRG) innovations of 1984, but unregulated sectors such as psychiatric hospitals, outpatient surgery, and home care were growing at dangerous rates of increase. Watching capitalistic forces find and invest massively in the unregulated components drew me to the realization that health expenditure and outcome improvement would not be achieved through regulation . . . but if financial incentives were aligned with health outcomes, outcome improvement would be achieved in ways impossible to predict and imagine.

It was at this same time that my idea for a sabbatical year to explore purchasing health outcomes began to emerge. I was, of course, aware of Paul Ellwood's and Al Tarlov's seminal medical outcomes thinking but had not seen evidence of using it to improve health status and outcomes at the population level. Two articles stimulated my thinking most in this period. The first was Steve Shortell's 1992 article, "A Model for State Health Reform," which presented a concept in which epidemiological measures of health status would guide health investment at the local and state levels. It was written, however, in the context of national health care reform and was quite vague on how the actual financial incentives might work. The other was the 1990 article by Bob Evans and Greg Stoddart, "Consuming Health Care, Producing Health," which inspired in me a sense of awe and discovery as they convincingly drew together many streams of research and experience in laying out the multiple determinants of health. I was privileged to be able to use draft chapters of the subsequent book *Why Are Some People Healthy and Others Not? The Determinants of Health of Populations* (Evans, Barer, and Marmor 1994) to teach two classes of graduate students in administrative medicine, an experience that convinced me to spend part of my sabbatical in Vancouver. I have an enormous personal and intellectual debt to Bob Evans, Morris Barer, and Clyde Hertzman and their colleagues in Canada, which will be evident to all who read this book.

It was clear to me from the outset that population health outcomes purchasing would depend on adequate measures of health status; having watched the impact of strong financial incentives at Montefiore and at the Medicare Prospective Payment Commission, I was respectful of their power as well as their potential for abuse. It occurred to me then (and I still think) that if Diagnostic Related Group creep resulted from Medicare Prospective Payment (as hospitals adjusted their diagnosis codes to higher payment categories), then population health outcome creep could be profound and problematic if one-seventh of the economy became oriented to this purchasing standard. Clearly outcomes measurement theory and technique was something I needed to know more about.

On the advice of Dan Fox at Milbank Memorial Fund and Steve Schroeder at Robert Wood Johnson Foundation, I met Alan Maynard, who was then the director of the Centre for Health Economics at the University of York in northern England. I spent the first six sabbatical months at York studying work on quality adjusted life years that began there in the early 1970s. I can never repay Alan Maynard, Alan Williams, Trevor Sheldon, and Wendy Taylor for their friendship during this period. Alan Williams provided me with a wealth of intellectual stimulation and new ideas and concepts. In particular, his early work with Tony Culyer (Williams 1974) on need for health being defined as "capacity to benefit" was eye opening and stimulating to a U.S. citizen who had come to believe that supply, demand, and ability to pay were all that health economics had to offer. I am also indebted to David Hunter and Gerald Wistow at the Nuffield Institute in Leeds for information regarding community care and joint commissioning in Great Britain.

Living in the United Kingdom and Canada for six-month periods provided invaluable insights about the cultural and historic rationale for how we approach and solve problems in the United States. Filling in for Victor Sidel at a seminar at the Karolinska Institute in Sweden on U.S. health care reform, I was momentarily silenced by the question, "What is the social and political philosophy underpinning the U.S. health care system?" After a minute of thought, I responded, "We actually don't do things that way . . . we mainly operate through technical innovation." The cross-national political analysis by Seymour Martin Lipset in his 1996 *American Exceptionalism: A Double-Edged Sword* was timely and meaningful in this regard, aiding an understanding of our more individualistic and less communitarian approach to social and economic policy. It helped me consolidate my thinking about the reasons for the failure of the Clinton Health Security Act and reinforced my managerial instincts that a more technical purchasing standard would have a much greater chance of realistic implementation than a massive, centralized, national program.

In addition to those already cited, I wish to thank Victor Sidel at Montefiore Hospital and Medical Center, Bronx, New York, for early encouragement and direction. My colleagues at the University of Wisconsin Department of Preventive Medicine have made contributions to my thinking and this book in many and varied ways; they include Denny Fryback, Colleen McHorney, Nancy Dunham, Jay Noren, John Mullahy, Barbara Wolfe, Mark Sager, Dan Wikler, Rocky Schulz, Don Kettl, Jim Sykes, Don Libby, and Donn D'Alessio. Chancellor Donna Shalala provided early encouragement as well, and the first statement of this thinking was published at her request in the September

1992 "Uncommon Wisdom" column of the *Wisconsin Alumni Magazine* as "The Health Care System Should Produce Health." Others read all or part of the book at various points and changed and added to my thinking; these include Don Detmer, Bill Roper, Bob Graham, Doug Conrad, Jo Boufford, Fitzhugh Mullan, Dan Fox, Harry Peterson, Howard Zuckerman, Steve Shortell, Dennis Prager, Roger Schenke, Phil Lee, and Steve Schroeder. I am particularly indebted to Colin Day, Bernie Cohen, Gary Filerman, Geoff Anderson, and Paul and Helen Kindig for reading and editing the entire manuscript. I was aided by high quality clerical and library assistance from Janet Sailor, Sarah Justus, and Michele Wuetrich, and by Rhonda Dix and Diana Western in medical illustration. My effectiveness in my varied professional activities is directly related to the dedication and commitment of my assistant, Penny Anderson, who kept things going and organized at Wisconsin during my year abroad, and who coordinated a variety of editorial tasks including the index.

I want to express special appreciation to my editor, Rebecca McDermott, at the University of Michigan Press. I will never forget my amazement as I was beginning to look for publishers at finding a letter from her asking if I knew of authors writing in the population health area. Her encouragement, criticism, friendship, and love of Big Ten basketball have made the final effort more human and no doubt of better quality.

Finally, this project would not have been possible without the love and support of my spouse and partner, Mary Norton Kindig, over the past 35 years and during this past year and a half. She helped immeasurably in the occasional loneliness of living elsewhere and also when the task of writing became discouraging. Her involvement in British and Canadian community life added considerable richness to my appreciation of these experiences. She has written a previous book, *Coping with Alzheimers Disease and Other Dementing Illnesses,* and as a social worker has made many complex medical ideas more understandable to her clients. Any idea that was not clear to her has been removed or explained better, and if the book is understandable to a nonacademic audience, much of the credit is hers.

Almost none of the original ideas on which this book builds are my own, but rather, they have been drawn from a wide variety of individuals, sources, and disciplines. My contribution has been to try to integrate all these concepts and experiences into a broad argument. I take full responsibility for whether it reflects the truth and provides accurate and realistic guidance for improving population health outcomes.

Contents

Acronyms

ADL	activities of daily living
ADA	Americans with Disabilities Act
CDCP	Centers for Disease Control and Prevention
DRG	Diagnostic Related Groups
DALY	disability adjusted life years
FAACT	Foundation for Accountability
GDP	gross domestic product
HEDIS	health plan employer data and information set
HALE	health adjusted life expectancy
HCFA	Health Care Financing Administration
HMO	health maintenance organization
IOM	Institute of Medicine
IADL	instrumental activities of daily living
JACHO	Joint Commission for the Accreditation of Healthcare Organizations
NCHS	National Center for Health Statistics
NCQA	National Committee for Quality Assurance
NHS	National Health Service (Great Britain)
OEO	Office of Economic Opportunity
OECD	Organization of European Cooperation and Development
PHS	Public Health Service (United States)
QALY	quality adjusted life years
SHMO	social health maintenance organization
WHO	World Health Organization
YHL	years of healthy life

1 · Purchasing Population Health: A Vision

We get paid for what we do, not what we accomplish.
  —Philip Lee, M.D., 1995

The health care industry is a $900+ billion endeavor that
does not know how to measure its main product: health.
  —Dennis Fryback, 1993

The Fundamental Argument

Despite the massive resources it consumes, the U.S. health care system
remains under stress. While we are global leaders in technical accom-
plishments in medicine, the amount of health we achieve per dollar
invested is far from optimal. So far, both market and regulatory reforms
have failed to address or even acknowledge this reality. The fundamental argument of this book, drawing from many disciplines such as medicine, economics, sociology, ethics, and management, is that we will not
maximize the amount of health we achieve until a measure of health
outcome becomes the purchasing standard for both the private and public sectors.

Our Health Expenditures Are the Highest in the World

Most Americans are now aware of the high costs of health care, if not
from their own payment experience, then from the barrage of print and
television coverage about major reorganizations in hospitals and insurance plans. As a percent of our gross domestic product (GDP), health
care spending has increased from 5.0 percent in 1960 to 13.6 percent in
1993 and 1995; similar 1993 figures for other countries were 10.2 percent in Canada, 8.6 percent in Germany, 7.3 percent in Japan, and 7.1
percent in Great Britain (USDHHS 1996). In terms of total health spending per person, this translates into $3,331 in the United States, $1,971 in
Canada, $1,815 in Germany, $1,495 in Japan, and $1,213 in Great
Britain.

In any other industry, this would be viewed as a miracle of
economic growth. Why not in health care? First, high health expenditures in relation to our international competitors could raise the prices
of our goods; an often cited example is that when a car is manufactured
in Detroit, health benefits cost more than the price of the steel. Related to
this is the impact on employee wages, since employers are not able to

give significant wage increases when health benefit costs are inexorably rising.

In addition, since health expenditures are approximately 46 percent from public sources (mainly Medicare and Medicaid), "automatic" increases in these programs decrease the amounts available for other public programs such as education, the environment, public safety, or tax reduction. Every state legislator understands the major tension between state expenditures for Medicaid and for public education. If the United States had similar per capita health expenditures as, for example, Germany in 1991, we would have had about $300 billion available in that year for alternate expenditures and/or lowered taxes. Over the past 25 years, neither regulatory nor market forces have been able to make a consistent or long lasting impact on these continuing increases in health expenditures.

Our Outcomes Are Lower than Expected

What about the quality and performance of the U.S. health care system? One would expect that our high level of expenditures would result in a population that is healthier than those of other countries that spend less. While it is true that our technology and specialized care are probably the best in the world, it is not appropriate to automatically conclude either that our population has better health or that further increases in health expenditures will make us healthier. In 1992, the United States ranked twenty-second in the world in infant mortality, twenty-fourth in male life expectancy at birth, and eighteenth in female life expectancy at birth. In 1994, it was identified by the World Bank as the nation with the worst health outcomes in relation to expenditures (USDHHS 1996). One study reported that 14–27 percent of deaths in 12 hospitals could have been prevented (Dubois and Brook 1988). Furthermore, within our country, there is great variation in health outcomes across states and communities. Figure 1 shows the complete lack of relationship between a composite measure of state health and state health expenditures.

This figure shows that total (private and public) state health expenditures per person range from $2,069 in Idaho to $3,892 in Massachusetts (Levit et al. 1995). In the same year, state health rankings ranged from 10 in Mississippi to 90 in Minnesota on the Northwest National Insurance Company Index reported annually in the national press (Northwestern National Life 1993). High expenditure states do not all have high health scores, nor do low health score states necessarily have low health expenditures. This relationship between expenditures

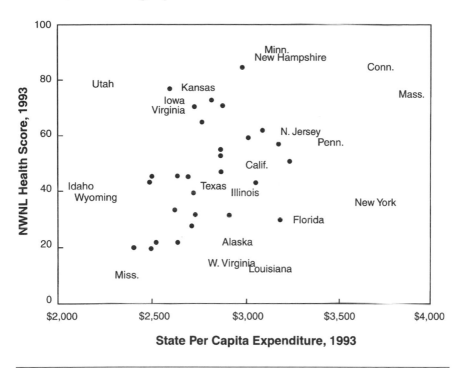

FIG. 1.   State health expenditure and health, 1993.
(Data from Health Care Financing Administration 1996. Northwestern National Life Insurance Company 1993.)

and outcomes is rarely, if ever, considered in private or public health care purchasing decisions.

We Have Change, Not Reform

Do failed federal or current market-based efforts warrant the term *reform*? While the 1994 Clinton Health Security Act would have guaranteed universal access and regulated cost increases, it was largely silent on improving health outcomes. In the wake of its defeat, major changes are taking place in the organization of the U.S. health care system through the growth of managed care and consolidated health care systems. Many people have concluded that the restructuring we are currently experiencing is, in fact, health care reform, without accompanying national leadership or legislation. These are indeed significant changes that are causing major challenges for providers and patients alike. But it is doubtful that they warrant the designation of *reform*, if this term continues to mean containing costs, increasing quality, and covering the uninsured.

Although many of the long-standing problems we face are sometimes blamed on health care providers, most hospitals and physicians are responding rationally to the financial incentives for providing more services under fee-for-service financing. Since providers are paid for each service in a fee-for-service environment, offering more services becomes the implicit output. On the other hand, in a managed care environment, capitation (annual cost per person) incentives create pressures for fewer hospital days, reduced physician services, and lower unit prices but do not yet require direct measures of health outcomes for health plan enrollees.

The Vision of Change: From Today to Tomorrow

This book proposes a Purchasing Population Health framework to guide twenty-first century health care purchasing for improved health outcomes. It argues that improving the public's health at prices we can afford cannot and will not be achieved until basic financial and managerial mechanisms and incentives are aligned to measures of health outcomes such as the length of and healthy related quality of life. The difference between this approach and our current system will become clear as we consider two imaginary communities, "Presentville 1997" and "Healthopolis 2020."

A Look at the Present: Presentville 1997

Financing
At the current time, Presentville's health care is financed by a combination of public and private payers, among them Medicare for the elderly, Medicaid for the poor, employers for many employed persons, and the self-employed (in some instances) for themselves. There are an increasing number of uninsured, mainly the working poor, whose employers do not provide health care benefits. While in many communities fee-for-service payment still dominates, it is gradually being replaced by capitation, in which providers or provider systems (hospital and physician plans) contract with Medicare, Medicaid, or employers to provide care that an individual or family will use for a year at a fixed predetermined rate. Competition among such systems is causing rate increases to employers to slow, but some are dropping individuals from coverage or

types of coverage and/or increasing the amount of out-of-pocket charges paid by individuals. It would be naive to think that this system does not ration care in largely silent and invisible ways.

Health Care Providers

Some freestanding hospitals and solo physician practices continue, but more and more hospitals and physician practices are merging into hospital systems and group practices and many into integrated hospital-physician systems. Some home health care is becoming integrated as well, but other components such as nursing homes and dentistry remain as separate components of the system. State and local public health agencies continue to provide, under increasingly constrained budgets, infectious disease, environmental, and restaurant surveillance as well as some basic personal services to the uninsured. Some discussion of integrating public health and private medical care is taking place but with little real progress.

Health Care Quality and Outcomes

The growth of managed care plans is stimulating concern about the quality of health care, particularly in the for-profit sector. This is largely because the profit incentives in capitation encourage providing fewer services, but ironically the concern about quality does not affect existing fee-for-service transactions to the same degree. Prevention and screening programs are increasing. National standards for measuring the quality of care in managed care plans are being refined and used in competitive advertising, but such measures do not yet adequately tell purchasers or patients which plans have better outcomes. For example, the percentage of women receiving Pap smears for cervical cancer may be reported but not whether the smears were read, whether the patients were appropriately treated, whether fewer cases of cervical cancer resulted, or whether cervical cancer death rates fell. State insurance commissioners are discussing what cost and quality data might be required at the state level, but no commonly accepted standards have emerged.

Nonmedical Determinants of Health

Other public and nonprofit sector functions that have an important impact on health such as social services, education, employment, and the environment are essentially independent and unrelated efforts, under fragmented rules and budgets, and funded or operated by different levels of government.

A Look at the Future: Healthopolis 2020

Under the Purchasing Population Health framework that this book advocates and envisions, how might this situation be different in another U.S. community, Healthopolis, in the year 2020?

Financing

Fee-for-service financing is a thing of the past. The nature of payment has been significantly revised, and it is this change in incentives that has driven broad provider integration. All health plans are now paid an annual capitation fee for their enrolled members, either by employers or by Medicare/Medicaid. Whereas in Presentville these payments were not related to health status, they now reflect both the health status and health need of the population covered; there are bonus incentives for those systems with the greatest improvement in outcome over time. It is possible that the communities in poorest health will attract relatively more new resources, since more improvement in health outcome per dollar is possible. Savings from providing only care that improves outcomes have been used in part to provide basic insurance benefits to all.

Health Care Providers

The consolidation of hospitals and physicians into local systems has been completed, and the remaining elements of the old medical care system such as long-term care, home health care, dentistry, and all drugs and equipment are now incorporated. Most communities are served by several competing health plans, so that annual patient choice based on performance as well as on cost is the rule. Public health agencies no longer provide personal health care since everyone is insured, but they continue to serve the public by assuming performance monitoring responsibilities.

Health Care Quality and Outcomes

A new indicator, called HALE (health adjusted life expectancy), a combination of length of life, disease, and disability, is the standard under which payment is now made to health plans. Data for such a measure is collected by provider systems, under regulation and review by state public health and insurance commissioners. Outcome data is available to the public to guide their choice of health care systems. New professional standards derived from such incentives are built into professional practice and medical education, and a continuous spirit of innovation for further improvement pervades practice and health research. Much of the concern about for-profit managed care has abated, since clear outcome and quality accountability has been established. Variation in health outcomes across subpopulations has significantly decreased.

Reinvestment of Savings
In Healthopolis 2020, the financing mechanisms proposed have slowly but steadily eliminated ineffective services and programs, with significant resources saved for alternative investments. The first investment was to supply small employers with matching funds to provide health insurance for all employees; the number of employees without health insurance has dropped to almost zero.

Nonmedical Determinants of Health
Most recently in Healthopolis, over the decade from 2010 to 2020, the understanding that health outcomes derive not only from medical care but from other social investments such as education, social services, employment, and the environment is being addressed. Private-public dialogue and new forms of cross-sectoral relationships, called Health Outcomes Trusts, are developing at the state and community levels in order to achieve the most cost-effective resource allocation. In many communities, resources saved from medical care that has not improved outcomes (no benefit or minuscule benefit per dollar) are being channeled into expansion of appropriate educational, employment, environmental, and social service initiatives. These, in turn, are contributing in part to improved health outcomes, as well as providing their own intrinsic benefits. In addition, ineffective investments in all health related sectors have been examined and are being eliminated.

A Realistic Vision

This approach has significant potential for stimulating improvement in health outcomes per dollar invested, through an intervention that is basically technical in nature and therefore more consistent with U.S. values and approaches (Lipset 1996). **It requires or envisions no new sweeping national legislation and no massive new bureaucracy.** It will appeal to conservatives and liberals, as well as to patients, health professionals, business executives, and legislators. It is not primarily a social or political proposal but more analogous to the acceptance of a new purchasing standard such as miles per gallon for a new car or the speed of a computer chip. As a tool in contract negotiations between purchasers of health care and provider organizations, it provides outcome and cost-effectiveness information so that these transactions are based on health outcomes, not just lower costs. This is not to say that there will not be changes in resource distribution, but in a Purchasing Population Health framework these will be considerably more objective and open in contrast to the current framework, which is primarily subjective and political.

Many other proposed approaches have failed, in part because of the complexity of health care itself and in part because of the power of vested professional and corporate interests in maintaining the status quo.

> **Most well meaning interest groups and organizational initiatives have only marginal impact when powerful financial incentives do not require health outcome improvement. The "do nothing" option is occasionally appropriate, but in the case of U.S. health care in the late 1990s it will, at best, result in minimal changes in outcomes at similar levels of investment. At its worst, doing nothing will result in continued cost escalation with no improvement in health outcomes. The price of inertia is the lost opportunity for a more appropriate value oriented balance of investments across the multiple determinants of health.**

This book is written in the hope that it will stimulate active discussion and debate about Purchasing Population Health. Although this is not an idea that could be fully implemented in the short run, much of what is suggested here could be well under way by the second decade of the twenty-first century. A three-phase development and implementation effort is outlined here:

Phase 1 (1997–2000)	Debate, research, and demonstration
Phase 2 (2001–10)	Outcome based payment for integrated health delivery systems
Phase 3 (2011–20)	Integration of social/environmental and educational health determinants

What Follows

The large and diverse body of research and experience necessary to understand the need for change and the proposed approach is reviewed and distilled here but presented in a way that is accessible to readers who are not health policy and financing experts.

Chapter 2, Taking Our Temperature: How Healthy Are We? reviews more fully the evidence about the health status of Americans and analyzes current approaches to both quality and outcomes measurement. It argues that while many current efforts show promise, they are far from adequately developed for the purpose of population health management and improvement.

Chapter 3, The High Cost of Health Care: Are We Getting the Most for Our Money? presents the trends in health expenditures, the reasons for their increases, the failure of traditional market forces, the impact of managed care expansion, and the lack of relationship between health expenditures and health outcomes.

Chapter 4, Measuring Health Outcomes, discusses the complex issues of how we currently measure health outcomes and quality and proposes a measure of health adjusted life expectancy (HALE) as the new purchasing standard at the large population/community level. Some such standard is necessary for Purchasing Populating Health to work, and this chapter will describe potential specific measures.

Chapter 5, The Multiple Determinants of Health, presents the evidence that health outcomes are the result of both nonmedical and medical factors acting in concert and describes what is known about the contributions to better health not only of medical care but also of education, income, social support, genetics, the environment, and individual behavior. Possible biologic mechanisms for nonmedical factors are discussed.

Chapter 6, Can Rationing Be Rational? Balancing the Determinants of Health, reviews current thinking and approaches to determining cost-effectiveness and presents a health outcomes perspective on rationing resources. The hypothesis is advanced that a balanced investment portfolio across determinants is essential if optimal outcomes are to be achieved in a world of limited resources.

Chapter 7, Managing Boundaries, discusses what is known about integrating across organizational and sectoral boundaries from a business and public administration perspective and identifies potential mechanisms that would have to be developed for the successful implementation of phase 3.

Chapter 8, Different Populations, Different Needs? examines the issue underlying resource allocation to populations of varying initial health status and need for investment. The critical concept of need as "capacity to benefit" from investment is introduced. Criticism of outcome measurement and management as potentially discriminatory toward certain groups such as the elderly or disabled are addressed.

Chapter 9, Making It Happen, spells out in more detail how the three-phase implementation proposal could evolve, with concrete suggestions regarding financial mechanisms, accountability, and intersectoral coordination. Critical remaining research questions are also identified here.

Chapter 10, The Case for Action, the Price of Inertia, describes the need for such action and the price of inaction. It argues that we must begin the public-private dialogue about Purchasing Population Health now, since every year of delay is one in which resources are being allocated to less than optimal health outcomes.

The mission of this book is to explore these relationships and put forth a practical approach to change. Purchasing Population Health is a synthesis of medical care, public health, health economics, sociology, and modern management, with the goal of achieving the most health for every precious dollar spent. It argues that a specific outcome measure of population health status to guide investment is absolutely required for optimal health improvement and value in the early twenty-first century.

2 · Taking Our Temperature: How Healthy Are We?

As many people are dying from preventable causes each year in the United States as would die if three jumbo jets crashed every two days.
  —Lucien Leape, 1994

What Is Health?

In order to determine how healthy we are, we first need a definition of health. Answering the question, What is health? is a challenge. Concepts and definitions of health range from the broadly philosophical to the narrowly statistical. Part of the complexity stems from the everyday usage of the word *health.*

A Narrow Definition of Health

To most of us, being healthy or unhealthy is a part of life's routine and is most often related in our minds to the presence or absence of disease. Figure 2 shows this elementary concept, where disease is equivalent to ill health and the health care response offers cure and/or care (Evans and Stoddart 1990).

An Expanded Definition of Health

However, health goes beyond the simple concept illustrated in figure 2. In a frequently quoted statement, the World Health Organization defines health as "complete physical, mental, and social well-being, and not merely the absence of disease or injury" (World Health Organization 1978). While this has often been criticized for its breadth and the difficulties it poses in terms of both measurement and achievement, the dictionary definition is similarly broad, citing "state of being sound in body and mind" (*Webster's* 1976). There is no precise solution to this definitional issue, but modern thinking does support a concept of health that is more than the absence of disease but less than the breadth of complete well-being. An important central concept is that of function, being able to perform not only physically and mentally but in social and occupational roles as well. In expanding this idea, Evans and Stod-

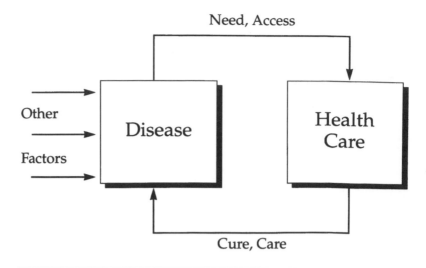

FIG. 2. Medical determinants of health model.
(Reprinted with permission from Evans, Robert G., et al. [eds.] *Why Are Some People Healthy and Others Not? The Determinants of Health of Populations* [New York: Aldine de Gruyter] Copyright © 1994, Walter de Gruyter Inc., New York.)

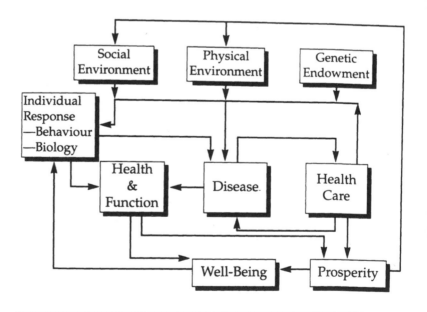

FIG. 3. Multiple determinants of health model.
(Reprinted with permission from Evans, Robert G., et al. [eds.] *Why Are Some People Healthy and Others Not? The Determinants of Health of Populations* [New York: Aldine de Gruyter] Copyright © 1994, Walter de Gruyter Inc., New York.)

dart develop a series of models more complex than figure 2 and arrive ultimately at the one shown in figure 3.

This model presents a definition broader than "disease"; it includes both "health and function" and "well-being," as well as a more complete view of the multiple determinants of health, encompassing interactions between medical care, the environment, socioeconomic status, genetics, and individual behavior. These multiple determinants of health will be covered extensively in chapter 5, but this expanded model is presented here to emphasize that a Purchasing Population Health framework requires the incorporation of all of these determinants.

How Healthy Are We?

Even with some general agreement and understanding of what is meant by health, answering the second question, How healthy are we? requires precise and useful measures.

The Length of Our Lives

The most common measure of the health of a population is that of mortality, not only because being dead precludes any concept of health but also because death rates are one of the most available and accurate health statistics. Mortality statistics are derived from death certificates and are recorded in the nation's vital statistics.

Overall mortality rates have been reported for decades, and therefore trends and comparisons over time and with other countries are available. Figure 4 illustrates the general improvement in mortality, expressed as the number of years someone born in a given year can be expected to live.

The trends are gradually upward (although not recently for some groups); such increases have occurred in the United States and in most developed countries over the last century. This increasing life expectancy is the result both of improvement in general socioeconomic conditions and public health and of advances in medical care. While advocates of one or the other cite contrasting evidence for their position, it is clear that the trend in improvement began before many of the miracles of modern medicine emerged. For example, figure 5 shows the decline in death rates from tuberculosis in relation to the historical development of treatment and preventive measures.

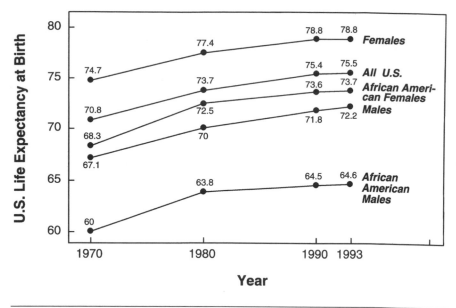

FIG. 4. U.S. life expectancy at birth.
(Data from USDHHS 1996).

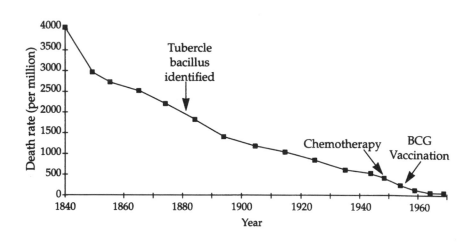

FIG. 5. Deaths from respiratory tuberculosis rates.
(From T. McKeown, *The Role of Medicine: Dream, Mirage or Nemisis?* 2d ed. [Oxford: Basil Blackwell, 1979]. Copyright © 1979 Basil Blackwell and Princeton University Press. Reprinted by permission of Basil Blackwell and Princeton University Press.)

TABLE 1.   U.S. Age Adjusted Death Rates

	1950	1970	1990
Total	840.5	714.3	520.2
White male	963.1	893.4	644.3
African American male	1,373.1	1,112.8	1,061.3
White female	645.0	501.7	369.9
African American female	1,106.7	814.4	581.6

Source: Data from USDHHS 1996.

Such evidence is not to be interpreted to mean that medical care is not important, but rather, it suggests that other factors have contributed to the decline in mortality. This point will be covered in detail in chapter 5.

Determining how healthy we are also requires a framework that provides an answer in comparison to some standard or benchmark. Comparisons can be made between different subgroups in a given country, such as men and women, racial and ethnic groups, or different geographic regions as illustrated in tables 1 and 2. Since age is a fundamental determinant of mortality, to insure comparability it is necessary to adjust mortality rates for age composition of any subgroup, in order to reflect the rates as if each one had identical proportions of persons of each age.

Table 1 shows the same trends as figure 4, using such mortality rates instead of life expectancy at birth. Total mortality has declined from 840 in 1950 to 520 in 1990; in each of these four subgroups declining mortality rates are seen, although from different starting points; in every case, females have lower mortality rates than men, and African Americans have higher rates than whites.

Table 2 compares age adjusted mortality across four geographic regions and five population classifications, according to degree of urbanization. The highest rate, 582, is in the northeast metropolitan core, and the lowest, 429, is in the west metropolitan fringe communities. This is a striking 36 percent variation in a very basic outcome measure. Rates in large metropolitan areas are higher than in rural areas, except for the south, where they are about the same, most likely due to the large African American rural population. In general rates are highest in the northeast and lowest in the west. The purpose here is not to explain these differences but to demonstrate the large variations in this basic health outcome indicator and to ask whether these variations are ever

TABLE 2.   U.S. Age Adjusted Death Rates

	Northeast	South	Midwest	West
Large metro core	582	564	569	491
Large metro fringe	459	467	466	429
Medium/small metro	478	529	483	475
Urban nonmetro	483	568	477	485
Rural	482	569	487	471

Source: Data from USDHHS 1996.
Note: Death rates are deaths per 100,000 resident population.

considered when medical care payment rates are determined or other health resources allocated.

U.S. Mortality Rates: A National Shame

Another comparative framework is between countries. While it is important to be certain that cross-national data are comparable, death rates among developed countries meet this standard. Table 3 shows how the United States ranks with selected other countries with respect to male and female life expectancy at birth.

According to this 1992 data, the United States is in 18th place with 79.1 expected years for a female, while U.S. males rank 23rd at 72.3 years (the table does not include all ranked countries). Although it is not possible to precisely explain these cross-national differences, U.S. performance clearly invites analysis and attention since considerably higher levels of life expectancy have been achieved elsewhere. Comparative mortality rates are sometimes criticized as not being "fair" because they contrast nations with substantial differences in their socioeconomic statuses or higher levels of minority populations associated with poorer health. In the full population health model developed in this book, such differences are seen as essential descriptions of the total outcome desired across the entire population. Examining cause-specific mortality rates can be helpful when looking for potential for improvements. For example, in many developed countries, death rates from heart disease are declining over time while those from accidents, homicides, and AIDS are increasing.

Quality of Life: Morbidity and Disability

Mortality data by itself is not an adequate operational definition of health. As Charles Dickens wrote, "It concerns a man more to know the

TABLE 3. Female and Male Life Expectancy at Birth, 1992

	Female	Rank order	Male	Rank order
Japan	83.0	1	76.3	1
France	82.3	2	73.8	11
Canada	81.4	4	74.9	3
Sweden	81.1	5	75.5	2
Australia	80.8	6	74.8	4
Spain	80.7	7	73.4	13
Norway	80.5	8	74.2	9
Italy	80.5	9	73.7	12
Greece	80.0	11	74.7	5
Finland	79.6	12	71.7	25
England/Wales	79.5	14	73.9	10
Germany	79.3	15	72.7	20
United States	79.1	18	72.3	23
Portugal	78.2	24	70.7	27
Cuba	76.8	29	72.9	17
Chile	76.5	30	69.4	30
Poland	75.8	32	66.7	33
Russian Federation	73.3	35	62	36

Source: Data from USDHHS 1996.

risk of 50 illnesses that may throw him on his back than the possible date of the one death that must come" (Brooks 1995). Measures of health that go beyond death rates are indicators of morbidity or disability. *Morbidity* is defined as pertaining to disease while *disability* refers to incapacity, particularly in the performance of everyday tasks and roles. The Americans with Disabilities Act of 1990 defined disability as a "physical or mental impairment that substantially limits one or more of the major life activities."

Measuring morbidity or disability is less precise than measuring mortality and is now only done for samples of the population. Several surveys such as the National Ambulatory Care Survey and the Health and Nutrition Examination Survey report periodically on the number of medical conditions and diagnoses in the population and compare trends over time. Initial measures of disability were primarily the number of days in bed and/or days of restricted activity as well as the number of persons with long-term limitations due to chronic illness. Since 1982, the National Long Term Care Survey has followed disability in terms of limitations in activities of daily living such as eating, bathing, toileting, shopping, housework, and mobility.

Standards or comparison groups for morbidity and disability

trends are more limited than for mortality. Most existing measures focus on a particular disease or physical function, although the activity limitation approaches described previously go beyond such a narrow focus. There is growing agreement that the outcomes of health care need to reflect both mortality and morbidity and disability, even though adequate measures of the latter are not yet routinely available for all populations.

Measuring Quality and Outcomes

Over the last several years we have seen more attention to the issues surrounding health care quality than ever in our history. For example, a 1997 headline in the "Money" section of *USA Today* states, "Businesses Leery of Health Care Quality" (*USA Today* 1997). Ironically, this attention has been fostered in part through the growth of managed care plans, where information on the quality and outcomes of care of populations is potentially available. President Clinton has appointed a National Advisory Commission on Consumer Protection and Quality in the Health Care Industry to report in early 1998 on quality and results of medical care and standards for consumer protection (*New York Times* 1996). Why is all of this necessary? Why aren't we more certain of what health care quality and outcome are?

Health professionals and health care institutions are concerned about both the quality of care they render and the outcomes of services for their patients. Such attention is increasingly built into the professional training and ethics of clinicians and managers and is reinforced by external agents in society. The rigor of medical education is the primary determinant of the quality of care, strengthened by requirements for continuing education and recertification. State licensure laws and malpractice claims are additional measures that establish minimal standards of quality. Hospitals have quality review committees and are required to be accredited every two years by the Joint Commission for Accreditation of Healthcare Organizations in order to receive Medicare and other payments. Nursing homes and home care agencies are also subject to periodic reviews. State insurance commissioners collect and report on a wide variety of statistics about the health care system within their jurisdictions.

There have been calls for moving to a more performance based approach to health system quality, most compellingly in Paul Ellwood's 1988 Shattuck Lecture on "Outcomes Management: A Technology of Patient Experience" (Ellwood 1988). Out of this has grown a significant body of work including his Outcomes Management System which sets forth a set of generic and condition-specific measurement tools to be used for feedback to clinicians and patients. From this work has emerged the Foundation for Accountability (FACCT), a new independent not-for-profit organization founded in 1995 by consumer groups, large private employers, and government agencies and dedicated to "improving the type of information consumers receive to make decisions about their health care." This organization is making important contributions to future generations of outcome measurements (Lansky 1996). The Medical Outcomes Study and the Medical Outcomes Trust of Tarlov, Ware, and colleagues have provided major stimulus and leadership to outcomes measurement approaches and research (Tarlov et al. 1989; Tarlov 1996). In addition to these efforts, Medicare has had a number of quality measurement and research initiatives under way for years (Jencks 1995), such as its Beneficiary Health Status Registry and its more recent proposal for Beneficiary-Centered Purchasing in the Medicaid managed care program (HCFA 1996).

While these efforts are for the most part invisible to the public, recent managed care "report cards," mainly fueled by the growth in managed care systems and the need for some standard of quality beyond the hospital setting, have been well publicized. The most widely used current system is the Health Plan Employer Data and Information Set (HEDIS), developed by the National Committee for Quality Assurance (Iglehart 1996; HEDIS/Report Cards 1997). It has come to popular attention through recent press stories such as that on the cover of *U.S. News and World Report* in September 1996, shown in figure 6.

In this article an "HMO honor roll" of the health plans with the best scores was presented. This honor roll's current version contains more than 60 performance indicators covering quality, access and satisfaction, membership, finance, and management; these are covered in more detail in chapter 4. Although use of the HEDIS system is voluntary, more than 80 percent of managed care plans surveyed are reviewing it for use in whole or in part. In many cases, compliance with these standards is being used in advertising in today's competitive health care marketplace, as shown in figure 7.

The Limits of Current Quality Measures

What are the limitations of this approach? Why don't all of these efforts give us adequate benchmarks for what our health care expenditures are accomplishing?

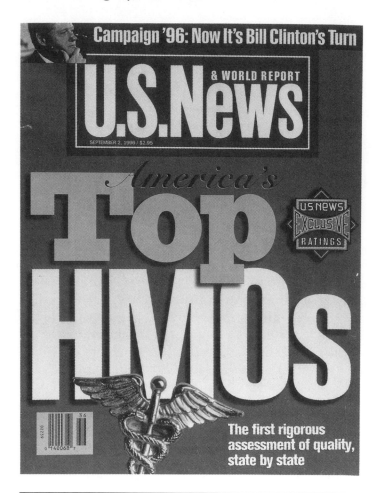

FIG. 6.   Reporting on HMO quality.
(Copyright, September 2, 1996, *U.S. News and World Report.*)

While the terms *quality* and *outcome* have so far been used almost interchangeably, they are not identical; outcome is critical to the entire argument in this book. One of the early scholars and pioneers of health care quality was Avedis Donabedian at the University of Michigan. In his early work, he identified three measurable components of quality: structure, process, and outcome (Donabedian 1980; see fig. 8).

Structure refers to basic inputs, such as the numbers of hospital beds, health care professionals, and medications needed to deliver health care services. Structural components are related to outcome

1996 Results

Oxford Health Plans Rated Highest.

Satisfaction with:	Oxford Health Plans' HMO and POS Rating	
• Health plan overall	#1	Major HMO and
• Choice of primary care physicians and specialists	#1	point-of-service (POS) plans in
• Care provided by primary care physicians and specialists	#1	Metropolitan New
• Satisfaction with primary care physicians and specialists	#1	York were rated in 10 key categories.
• Quality and reputation of hospitals	#1	Both Oxford's
• Quality of medical care	#1	HMO and POS plans finished first
• Customer service	#1	in all 10.
• Concern shown for health and well-being	#1	
• Likely to recommend plan	#1	Source: CareData Reports, Inc. 1996
• Likely to re-enroll in plan	#1	

FIG. 7. Marketing HMO quality.
(From CareData Reports Inc., 1996.)

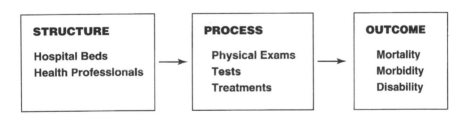

FIG. 8. Components of quality: structure, process, outcome.

since there would be no medical services at all without them. They are relatively easy to measure.

Process refers to procedures and interventions (such as tests, operations, patient education) whose purpose is to convert structural factors and resources into health results or outcomes. These can also usually be measured, and they are the major components of many of the quality reporting systems mentioned in the preceding pages.

Outcomes refers to the ultimate achievement of the system, such as the mortality and life expectancy rates shown previously, and goes beyond mortality to include measures of morbidity, disability, and quality of life.

The most widely used definition of quality at this time is one issued by a distinguished panel of experts for the Institute of Medicine in 1990. They concluded that

> **quality of care is the degree to which health services for individuals and populations increase the likelihood of desired health outcomes and are consistent with current professional knowledge.**

They stated that under such a definition, health care services are expected "to have a net benefit, with regard to patient satisfaction and well-being, health status and quality of life outcomes, and the process of patient-provider interaction and decision-making" (Lohr 1990).

Chapter 4 will go into much more detail about how health outcomes are measured. For now, suffice it to say that while the last decade has shown considerable concern and developmental work in outcomes and quality (Kassirer 1993; Blumenthal 1996), most attention has been at the process level, not the outcome level. Furthermore, this effort has focused primarily on individual patients and clinical units such as hospitals, not on larger populations or communities. This has been due in part to the dominance of "quality improvement" approaches derived from the work by Deming, which primarily focus on process improvement (Deming 1986; Berwick 1989).

> **While the purpose of such quality improvement and "report card" efforts is to assist purchasers, in practice no specific approach for linking process or outcome measures to financial incentives has been proposed.**

While structure and process are related to outcome, this relationship is incomplete enough to be an invalid basis for judging the overall performance of the system and the investments in it, certainly at the community or health plan level. While health professionals and institutions will say—and genuinely mean—that they are concerned about the ultimate health outcomes of their patients, they do not often have the available data systems to provide adequate outcome information. Further, the data available may be faulty or misinterpreted, and—in any event—they are not used to thinking about the outcomes for the large groups of patients who make up their practices.

Managed care systems and ambulatory networks are beginning to have data systems to collect such statistics, but they are not widely used either to judge performance or to consider alternative investment possibilities. In many cases, data has been collected without a specific purpose in mind, so it remains useless as information. State and national governments have both mortality and morbidity data, but since governments are not primarily responsible for patient care and financing, the connection between outcome and expenditure is rarely made. Until such integration is achieved, beginning attempts at reform will remain marginalized, either as genuine efforts by committed individuals and institutions or simply as a marketing approach by those who are satisfied to provide medical services without regard to ultimate outcome.

Summary

This chapter has demonstrated that while there is increased attention to health care quality in the United States, most of these efforts still focus on process (such as procedure rates and patient satisfaction) rather than outcome measures and leave private and public purchasers without adequate guidance with regard to health care investment decisions. Better measures for population health outcomes will be presented in chapter 4. But first the reasons for our very high health expenditures and what we know about the relationship between health expenditures and health outcomes will be explored.

3 · The High Cost of Health Care: Are We Getting the Most for Our Money?

Healthcare consumes 13.7 percent of our GNP. A fairer
system would make better use of the money we now spend,
and it would allow us to provide compassionate care to all
Americans.
—Richard Scott, former CEO of Columbia/HCA, 1996

It is one thing to assert that health outcomes are not being achieved as efficiently as they might be. It is another to design and implement a process that will improve them. In order to do so, it is first necessary to clearly understand how much we are spending, since efficiency requires consideration of outcomes achieved for resources expended. This chapter describes how health care costs are measured and what the trends in health expenditures have been. It analyzes why our health care is so expensive, why traditional market forces have had limited impact, and how recent managed care incentives have brought about change. Finally, evidence for the limited relationship between health expenditures and health outcomes is presented.

How Much Does Our Health Care Cost?

Health care in the United States accounts for one-seventh of our national economy, and it includes institutions and services that are of critical, often life and death, importance to the population. Many depend on the health care industry for jobs; one person's health expenditure is another's income. In many areas, both rural and urban, health care employment is critical to the economy of the area. For most individuals the system works, even though increasing numbers of people are calling for change because of insecurity about coverage or worry about costs. Changing the system by increasing coverage and/or decreasing costs requires a clear and compelling rationale or it will be met with resistance by patients and providers who are skeptical of change, particularly in the light of the failed Clinton plan. What we have may be flawed, but the unknown is more uncertain, and pragmatic caution or inertia reigns. As this chapter details current expenditures and their relationship to outcomes, the foundation for the fundamental argument of this book will become clear: we can achieve better outcomes for the resources we expend, but this will not happen until expenditures are aligned with health outcome expectations. To build outcomes into fundamental managerial and financial incentive structures, a health outcome purchasing standard is essential.

It is common knowledge that the costs of health care in the United States are high and increasing. We have all experienced the high price of hospital care, emergency room visits, medications, and nursing home care, whether or not insurance is available. We also know this because in the mid-1980s a public policy debate surfaced that focused attention on these costs over the past two decades. State and federal legislators were looking at "automatic" increases in public spending for Medicaid and Medicare created by price and volume increases, and employers were facing the growth in fringe benefit costs. Let us first answer two questions: (1) what have been the trends in national health expenditures? and (2) why have these increases happened?

How Are Health Expenditures Measured?

Keeping track of national health expenditures in the United States is complex, primarily because of the pluralistic nature of our system and the many different cost and revenue centers that it encompasses. It is the job of the Office of the Actuary in the federal Health Care Financing Administration to record and periodically report this data. This is relatively easy for public programs like Medicare and Medicaid where national and state figures are available. It is not so straightforward for nongovernmental expenditures through private insurance or out-of-pocket cash payments, since no such comparable central data source exists.

Instead a variety of individual data sources are used. For hospital care, data is obtained from the American Hospital Association survey of hospital revenues. For physician and dentist expenses, a sample of tax records from the Internal Revenue Service is used. Combining data from multiple sources, an annual report is produced by the Office of the Actuary of the Health Care Financing Administration (Levit et al. 1996), and this is shown in simplified form for 1995 as table 4. It demonstrates the most important health expenditure data for the U.S. health care system.

The vertical columns show the type of expenditure (such as hospital care or physician services), and the horizontal rows demonstrate the source of funds for that expenditure. The data shows that total national expenditures in 1995 were $989 billion. The columns below the total indicate the percent of total expenditure in each category. Hos-

TABLE 4.   National Health Expenditures 1995 (billions of dollars)

		Source of Funds			
Type of Expenditure	Total	Out of Pocket	Insurance	Other	Public
Total	989	183 (19%)	311 (31%)	39 (4%)	456 (46%)
Hospital	350 (35%)	11	113	11	214
Physician	202 (20%)	37	97	4	64
Dental	46 (5%)	22	22	0	2
Home health	29 (3%)	6	3	3	16
Drugs	83 (8%)	50	22	0	11
Nursing home	78 (8%)	29	3	2	45
Administrative	48 (5%)	0	34	1	13
Other	153 (16%)	28	17	18	91

Source: Data from Levit et al. 1995.

pitals received the largest share at $350 billion, 35 percent of the total. Physicians accounted for $202 billion or 20 percent, drugs for $83 billion or 8 percent, and nursing homes for $80 billion or 8 percent.

The columns across the top show both private and public sources of expenditures. Private cash outlays represented 19 percent of the total, private health insurance paid for 31 percent, and public programs (primarily Medicare and Medicaid) financed 46 percent. But this division of financing is not the same across all types of health expenditures. Whereas hospital expenditures are primarily divided between private insurance and public sources, items like drugs and nursing home care have much higher out-of-pocket cash outlays by individuals and families.

Trends in Health Expenditures

What has the growth in expenditures been over time? Costs can either be shown as total dollars or as per capita expenditures, but such numbers need to be adjusted for the overall price increases in the economy from inflation. It has become common for comparative purposes across time and across countries to report expenditures as a percent of the total gross domestic product, which incorporates the inflation factor. Figure 9 is now a familiar one, showing the growth from 7.4 percent in 1970 to 13.9 percent of GDP in 1994. For comparative purposes, the trends in expenditures for education are also presented over the same time period.

While the projections in figure 9 for 2000 and 2005 are the most recent ones from Burner and Waldo 1995, they may not have adequately

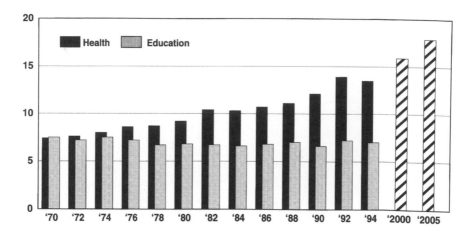

FIG. 9. Health care and education expenditures.
(Data from Health Care Financing Administration 1996. *Digest of Education Statistics,* U.S. Department of Health, Education, and Welfare, 1995.)

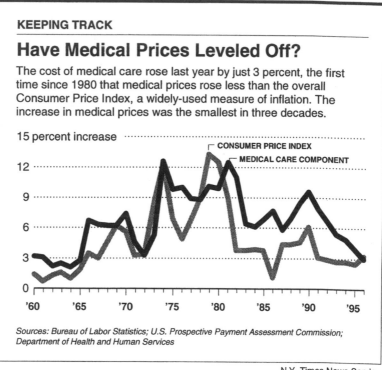

FIG. 10. Have medical prices leveled off?
(From *New York Times,* January 19, 1997. "Medicare Panel Advises a Freeze on Hospital Pay.")

accounted for the impact that managed care is having and perhaps need to be revised downward (Miller and Luft 1995). Under managed care incentives, rates that employers pay for their employees have begun to drop in many markets (Ginsburg and Pickreign 1996), and medical price inflation has fallen recently to 4 percent real growth in 1994, as shown in figure 10.

This figure shows that annual increases in the medical care component of the Consumer Price Index (CPI) have approached the general inflation rate for the first time since the late 1970s. This trend recently prompted the Medicare Prospective Payment Assessment Commission to recommend for the first time ever that Congress not increase payment rates to hospitals in 1997. However, at the same time, some employer benefits consultants began to advise in early 1997 that recent slowdowns are only temporary and that "high single digit or even double digit increases" are increasingly possible in 1998 and beyond (*New York Times* 1997).

How does the United States compare to other developed countries in this regard? While data comparability is an issue when crossing national expenditure systems, expenditures reported from the 13 developed countries in the Office of European Cooperation and Development are similar enough for accurate gross comparison. Figure 11 shows that while almost all countries are experiencing growth, the United

$ per capita

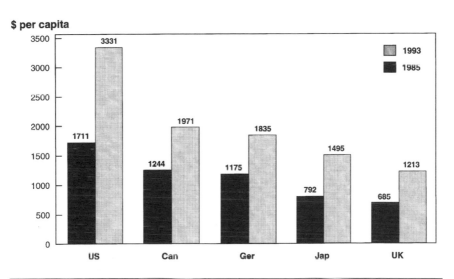

FIG. 11. Comparative health care expenditures.
(Data from USDHHS 1996.)

States leads the world both in per capita expenditures and in recent growth.

It is also interesting to examine the relative levels of health expenditure across the 50 United States. As seen previously in figure 1, in 1993 there was a twofold difference in total per capita expenditures across the states. Of course, states differ in characteristics such as wage rates, number of elderly, and number of persons who come into the state for expensive care. However, one analysis showed that these demographic factors accounted for only about one-third of the variation, with the remainder associated with other characteristics of the state health care environment such as the numbers of physicians and hospital beds (Kindig and Libby 1994).

Why Is Our Health Care So Expensive?

Price vs. Volume

The reasons for the increase in health expenditures are complex. Figure 12 shows the general factors responsible for growth since 1960.

While in some periods, such as 1970–80, economy-wide inflation dominated the picture, since 1980 medical care price inflation (over general inflation) was very significant, as was the large increase in intensity (volume of services per person) in 1990–91. When these rates of increase over general inflation rates continue, the percent of GDP devoted to health expenditures increases automatically as shown in figure 9.

Specific factors for the increase include the following: rising physician incomes, an excess of specialists, the aging of the population, paperwork and administration, "defensive medicine" in the malpractice climate, and new technology. All of these and more play a role. Figure 13 shows the rates of utilization of selected technologies between Canada, Germany, and the United States.

Lower rates are not necessarily better, since very low expenditures such as in the United Kingdom can result in waiting lines and possible underutilization. However, evidence exists that in the United States we are using more services than are effective in improving our overall health status.

A recent study comparing Canadian and U.S. physician expenditures indicated that Canadians received a higher volume of services for lower total expenditures, explained entirely by lower physician fees (Fuchs and Hahn 1990). Within the United States, the pioneering work

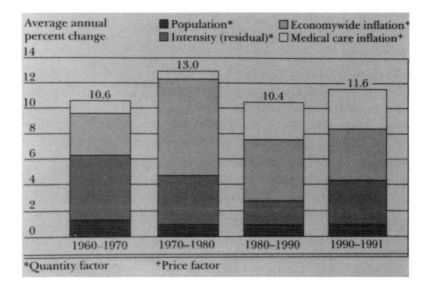

FIG. 12. Factors accounting for growth in personal health expenditures.
(Altman, S., and Reinhardt, U., *Strategic Choices for a Changing Health Care System* [Chicago: Health Administration Press, 1996], 7.)

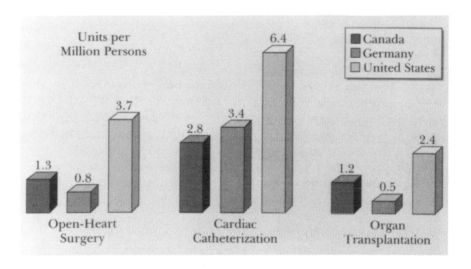

FIG 13. Comparative availability of selected medical technologies.
(Altman, S., and Reinhardt, U., *Strategic Choices for a Changing Health Care System* [Chicago: Health Administration Press, 1996], 22.)

of John Wennberg has pointed out the significant variation in the number of medical and surgical procedures, such as hysterectomies, in different areas of the country, even after correcting for underlying differences in illness rates (Wennberg and Gittelsohn 1982). In addition, an increasing number of studies are showing the extent of "inappropriate" or unnecessary care. Brook and colleagues recently said it this way:

> The current practice of medicine is far from perfect. One-fourth of hospital deaths may be preventable, and one-third of some hospital procedures may expose patients to risk without improving their health. One-third of drugs may not be indicated, and one-third of abnormal laboratory tests may not be followed up by physicians. (Brook, Kamberg, and McGlynn 1996)

While considerable research and clinical attention are focusing on finding these variations and correcting any inappropriate medical interventions, the absence of clear health outcome measures limits the effectiveness of traditional economic forces in achieving this goal.

Could a new purchasing standard assist purchasers, providers, and patients alike to increase the effectiveness of market forces by "paying for results"?

"Market Failure" in Health Care

There is often confusion about why economic principles that work in other sectors of the economy do not carry over to the health care sector. For example, if the supply of hospitals or doctors increases, prices do not fall. There are several reasons for the so-called market failure in health care, but the main one of relevance here is the lack of perfect information between customer and seller. Someone buying a car can obtain fairly complete information about the product from inspection, advertising, consumer magazines, and a test drive. Even repair records from past years' models are available, and good information about reasonable prices exists.

The main reason for the difference in health care is the complex and scientific nature of medicine. Much of modern medicine is rooted in basic scientific principles that are not easily understood by those without appropriate training. Indeed, some aspects of complex drugs and procedures are not completely understood by physicians of another specialty. Currently there are major advances in the amount of information available to consumers, increasingly in electronic interactive form.

Although the role of the patient in his or her own health outcome improvement has increased (see individual responsiblity section in chapter 5), it has not yet become a significant force in the marketplace.

Furthermore, much of medicine remains an art, in that precise rules and guidelines in many situations are neither available nor possible. For instance, one of the reasons for the variations in the number of surgical procedures in different regions of the United States is that there is a zone of uncertainty in many cases where clear indications do not exist and professional judgment necessarily takes over. Other examples of areas of professional uncertainty include such decisions as the age for mammography screening, whether or how to treat early prostate cancer, how often follow-up visits for chronic disease are needed, and drugs vs. psychotherapy for certain mental illnesses.

Another reason that market forces do not fully apply to medical care is that patients often do not want to be involved in the evaluation of their doctor or hospital in the same way they would when buying a new car or a brand of beer. Health care is personal and often of life and death importance, and the belief that someone else is in charge and knows best is frequently desired. This is reflected in survey results over time that indicate that Americans are critical of the health care system but not of their own providers. This is changing to some degree with better patient education materials and even interactive computer programs that allow patients to learn about their options and to indicate their preferences, particularly in areas of professional uncertainty. But to the extent that clear information to evaluate outcomes of medical care exists at all, it remains largely in the professional domain.

Yet another reason for the lack of influence of market forces is that health care professionals and institutions have not had either the tools or the incentives to develop outcome standards at the population level themselves. This statement is in no way intended to demean the intentions and motivations of health care clinicians and managers. With rare exceptions they are trained and committed to both high quality care and positive outcomes for their patients, and of course obtaining good outcomes at the individual clinical procedure level is commonplace (setting a fracture or treating pneumonia). But data about what has worked for many different patients over time in varied, complex circumstances is not routinely available, and memory and anecdote are imperfect. New computer technology will aid in this in the future, but in many cases outcome information simply does not exist, and often long-term follow-up is not possible.

Current Economic Incentives in Health Care

For many years, financial incentives have favored doing more rather than less, since under a fee-for-service system each additional visit or test or operation yields additional income to the clinician and/or institution. It is not surprising that physicians and hospitals behave as rational economic actors, providing more and more services, particularly in areas of professional uncertainty. Indeed, such incentives are to a considerable degree responsible for the increase in the volume of services and health expenditures seen previously.

Recently, however, both regulatory and market based reforms have begun to reverse these fee-for-service incentives. For hospital payment, Medicare reforms in 1984 introduced the Prospective Payment System, which pays hospitals for an entire admission rather than for each day of a hospital stay. This system created more than 400 Diagnostic Related Groups (DRGs), which bundled all days and tests for each category of treatment into a single standard rate and created incentives for fewer days as well as for looking carefully at the tests and other services provided during the admission (Altman and Ostby 1991). In business terms, this would be the equivalent of a fixed price contract instead of a cost plus contract.

But while DRG payments began to control costs within a hospital stay, they did nothing to control the number of admissions themselves. They also led to increased expenditures outside of the hospital such as for home care services. The advent of managed care takes such incentives another step, bringing both the volume and the price of services under scrutiny. Under managed care arrangements, doctors and hospitals in a coordinated system agree to provide all needed care to a group of employees or Medicare or Medicaid recipients for a specified rate per person (this is why the rates are called capitation rates) for a fixed period of time, usually a year (Luft and Morrison 1991). Managed care replaces the economic pressure for overutilization in fee for service with incentives to reduce utilization. Indeed, managed care plans generate most of their cost savings by reducing the number of hospital admissions per person.

The past decade has seen amazing growth in managed care plans, as shown in figure 14. While early growth was in the employer based insurance markets, currently 32 percent of Medicaid (Rowland and Hanson 1996) and 10 percent of Medicare (Welch 1996) recipients are enrolled in managed care plans. There are a large variety of such plans, ranging from not-for-profit tightly managed group-staff models

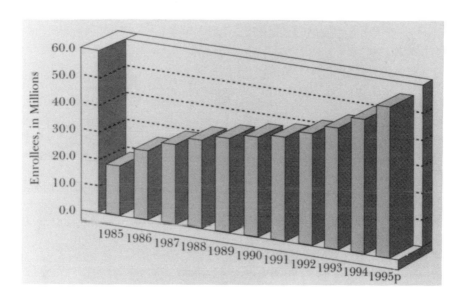

FIG. 14.   Enrollment in HMOs. 1995p is projected.
(Altman, S., and Reinhardt, U., *Strategic Choices for a Changing Health Care System.*
[Chicago: Health Administration Press, 1996], 45.)

(sometimes with community boards and salaried physicians) to for-profit loosely formed networks of physicians and hospitals, often run by insurance companies and held together through various contracts and agreements. These plans are certainly responsible for much of the recent slowing in health care cost increases described earlier.

Limits of Managed Care Incentives

However, even powerful managed care incentives have not dealt fully with the cost-containment issue for several reasons. The first is that even at 4 percent real growth, the share of GDP devoted to health care will continue to rise, if at a slower rate. It is unclear whether it is realistic to expect that the percent of GDP devoted to health can actually fall, although we have seen examples of other nations that have much lower levels of national resources devoted to health care.

Beyond the problem of actually reducing health expenditures as a percentage of GDP, there is the additional difficulty that many persons are still not in managed care systems or other types of systems that coordinate care more efficiently. Also, cost reductions are achieved not only by eliminating unnecessary services but also by decreasing benefits and/or by increasing co-payments to the patient for certain services such as medications and ambulatory visits. While this may lower the premiums that employers have to pay the managed care plans, it does not necessarily lower expenditures either to the individual or to the nation. Furthermore, in many managed care plans, only hospital and physician services are covered, leaving many components of health care outside the system. Finally, in many markets, competition between plans has led to duplication of equipment, facilities, specialists, and advertising in order to attract and keep patients in a particular plan.

But whatever the current limitations, it is generally agreed that economic incentives such as DRGs and managed care, which require providers and insurers to carefully examine their services and costs, have great potential for savings in the long run, certainly in comparison to the undisciplined fee-for-service incentives that are in large part responsible for the growth in health expenditures already described.

The Relationship between Health Spending and Health

Now that we have reviewed the fundamentals of U.S. health expenditures and health outcomes, how can we describe the nature of the relationship between the two? Is the U.S. population getting health value for its health care investments? Are the high and growing expenditures bringing a concomitant increase in health status? In other words, do higher investments produce better health? This is not a question that has been answered—at least not completely—by researchers in the field, because the relationship is complex and because the type and availability of data on health and health expenditures are imperfect.

Diminishing Marginal Return

Again the best evidence about the relationship between health status and health expenditures comes from international comparisons of health expenditures and mortality rates. Figure 15, taken from the World Bank's *World Development Report 1993: Investing in Health,* displays the relationship between per capita income and life expectancy for most countries of the world since 1900.

This figure demonstrates that there has long been a positive

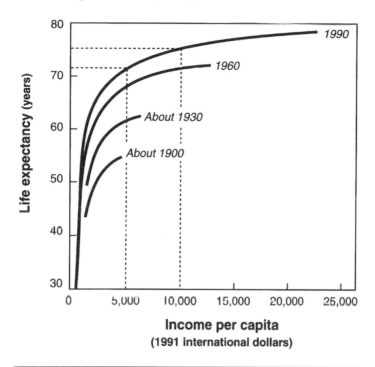

FIG. 15.   Income per capita vs. life expectancy.
(Adapted from World Bank, *World Development Report 1993: Investing in Health* [New York: Oxford University Press, 1993], 34.)

relationship between life expectancy and national per capita income but that a decreasing return begins to develop at higher expenditure levels (around $5,000 per capita in 1990). Diminishing marginal return is an important concept both in economics and in population health; it refers to lower increases in output for equivalent additional increases in input. In this figure on the 1990 line, the first $5,000 in per capita income is associated with about 72 years of life expectancy, while the second $5,000 ($5,000 to $10,000) is associated only with about 3 more years of life expectancy, from 72 years to 75 years.

That part of the line that has less increase in output is sometimes called the "flat of the curve" and is one of the most important concepts in thinking about the relationship between health expenditures and health outcomes. Of course, because the quality of data for low-income countries is not totally comparable with data quality for countries with higher incomes, only the general relationship can be demonstrated. Also, demonstrating such a relationship between these

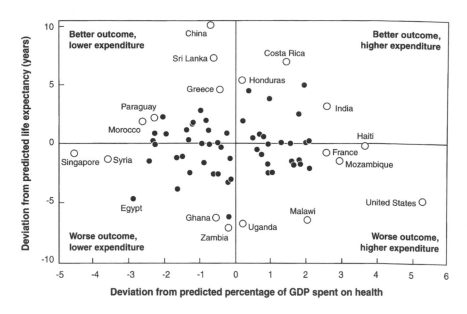

FIG. 16.   Health expenditure and life expectancy.
(From World Bank, *World Development Report 1993: Investing in Health* [New York: Oxford University Press, 1993], 54.)

two factors does not prove that one causes the other, certainly when multiple factors are involved.

Figure 16, also taken from the World Bank's *World Development Report 1993: Investing in Health,* demonstrates the relationships between health spending and life expectancy.

This figure plots countries in relation to their predicted life expectancy, given their level of health expenditures. Many of the countries fall in the middle of the graph and are therefore unnamed.

But those at the extremes of the quadrants are displayed, with the *United States uniquely identified as having the worst predicted outcome for the level of expenditure.*

Whatever the causal relationship between health spending and health status, it certainly varies across countries of profoundly different socioeconomic circumstances. Without formal analysis it is not difficult to accept the likelihood that investments in pure water and immunizations will greatly improve health status in very poor countries, while more complex and costly investments in medical care, prevention, and the environment are probably necessary for health outcome improve-

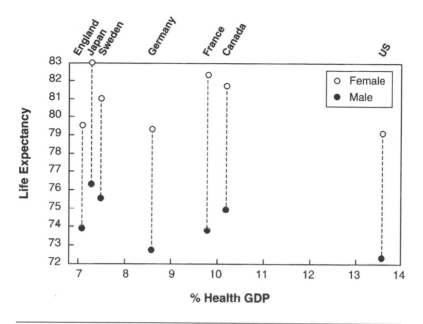

FIG. 17. Health expenditure and life expectancy, 1992.
(Data from USDHHS 1996.)

ment in the developed world (except for severely deprived settings in the inner cities of developed countries).

The concern of this book is with the United States, using similar developed countries as one point of comparison. Figure 17 shows a plot of male and female life expectancy at birth compared to the percent of GDP spent on health for several OECD countries.

This figure shows that there is no clear relationship between expenditures and life expectancy at birth, but the two outlier countries, the United States and Japan, are examples of an inverse relationship: higher expenditures associated with lower life expectancy for the United States and the opposite for Japan, indicating again that it may be possible for us to achieve better health results over the whole population without increasing the percentage of GDP devoted to health care.

Beyond Mortality Measures

As indicated earlier, mortality alone is a limited measure of health, and there is a paucity of data going beyond this measure. In the United States, every year the Northwestern National Life Insurance Company releases its profile of the relative health of the 50 states. Their measure of health is a weighted composite of 19 factors, including mortality from several causes (infant mortality, smoking rates, accident rates, etc.). Although this index requires validation by other researchers, it is usually picked up by national newspapers and is clearly in the public domain. Once again we find this cross-state data demonstrates no clear relationship between state health expenditure and this composite measure of health (see fig. 1).

So, there is a reasonable possibility that the United States is operating on the flat of the curve, that it could purchase more health at less cost, and that further overall increases in health care expenditures will have limited return in terms of health outcomes.

It is not being suggested here that there is a "correct" level of health expenditure as a percentage of GDP or some other economic or health care indicator. But the amount of resources involved in U.S. health expenditures at the flat of the curve is enormous. The evidence in this chapter shows that there is an opportunity to reduce the rate of growth in health expenditures, and even the absolute level over time, yielding savings for which a country with limited resources could find productive use, either in health care or in other sectors. Indeed, later chapters will argue that such alternate spending patterns might ultimately increase U.S. population health status.

Healthopolis 2020 Revisited

The vision of Purchasing Population Health described in our hypothetical future community in chapter 1 was to develop a link between health expenditures and health outcomes and to suggest financial incentives aimed at improving the outcome performance of the health of enrolled populations. There have been beginning discussions about making a twenty-first century paradigm shift to redefine the product of the health care system as population health status, and to create economic incentives in these integrated health care delivery systems and other health promoting sectors of society to produce health in the most cost-effective manner. However, only a few rudimentary proposals have been put forth, without specific financing or implementation plans (Birch and Maynard 1986; Eyles et al. 1991; Shortell 1992; Kindig 1993; Patrick and Erickson 1993; Ellwood and Lundberg 1996; Shortell et al. 1996), and financial incentives across the boundaries of other health enhancing sectors such as education and the environment have not yet been considered.

A Focus on Outcomes

A Purchasing Population Health framework would encourage the establishment of outcomes for each community or health plan; the goal would be to decrease mortality, morbidity, and disability as efficiently as possible.

> **In such a system, explicit financial incentives would be developed to ensure movement toward improvement of the health status of populations. Such a focus would turn attention to outcomes rather than structure or process and would unleash forces that would capture the attention of health providers, health institutions, and other health enhancing sectors of society that are currently not held accountable for such outcomes.**

It should reassure those concerned about managed care incentives for underutilization and "skimming" of profits, since agreed upon and accountable measures of performance would be in place; if for-profit plans could deliver equal or better risk adjusted outcomes than nonprofit or public providers and still return profit to shareholders, this policy concern might vanish. It would also stimulate a wide array of creative approaches to begin to make progress toward this new goal. Clearly defined goals provide an incentive in and of themselves in that satisfaction and fulfillment for effort exerted can be realized in a concrete way.

Summary

This chapter has discussed why some of our current health expenditures are so high and has argued that the lack of a clear outcome purchasing standard has limited the effectiveness of traditional market forces. Before considering what financial incentives could be developed, we need an objective measure of population health. Chapter 4 will review the current status of objective measures combining mortality and health care quality and identify several under development that could be appropriate for this purpose.

4 · Measuring Health Outcomes

I am fain to sum up with an urgent appeal for adopting this or some uniform system of publishing the statistical records of hospitals. If they could be obtained . . . they would show subscribers how their money was being spent, what amount of good was really being done with it, or whether the money was doing mischief rather than good.
—Florence Nightingale, 1863

Though varying in language and emphasis, their [leading economists'] responses came down to this: It's too hard to measure the things you're talking about. Each time they said this I would reply, "I know it's hard, but this doesn't mean it is impossible. If it's also important, why don't we get started?" We didn't get started then, and the task is even more important now. So why don't we get started now?
—Elliott Richardson, 1996

The concept of Purchasing Population Health requires financial incentives that encourage and reward improvement in health outcomes. This is fundamentally different from the current system that pays for medical care services and relies primarily on process measures of quality or on professional judgment alone as the measure of value that private or public purchasers and individual patients can expect from their investment. Reorienting one-seventh of the nation's economy to a revised standard of outcome is no small intervention, and therefore any new outcome measures must be carefully considered and developed.

The previous chapters have touched briefly on definitions of health outcome. This chapter focuses in more depth on two basic questions:

What is the definition of health?" and
"How can it be measured?

It summarizes a large amount of technical information but in a way that is accessible and clear. It is organized into four sections:

· Defining Population Health
· Measuring Health Adjusted Life Expectancy (HALE)
· A Single Measure: The Gross National Health Product?
· The Tyranny of Outcomes?

Defining Population Health

Population health is a term that is increasingly used but ill defined. Often it is incorrectly thought of as synonymous with public health, prevention, or primary care, but these are limited definitions for this purpose since they do not encompass the broad and complete concept of health presented earlier. Certainly the population-based interventions of public health such as community health education and fluoridation of water are included, but much relevance is done in both the nonprofit and for-profit private sectors. Health promotion and disease prevention as well as primary care are critical components, but many aspects of health improvement come from diagnosis and treatment in secondary and tertiary care as well.

The first step is to distinguish between the concepts of health and population health. Regarding health itself, in the simple model presented in figure 2 (chap. 2), disease was the negative definition of health, and health care was the appropriate and only response to this aberration. Figure 3 presented a much more complete population health model, with the additional determinants referred to throughout this book. In the second model, while health care and disease are still present in the feedback loop, two other health concepts, (1) health and function and (2) well-being, have been added. As before, disease is considered to be biologic dysfunction, diagnosed by medical professionals and/or technology. The idea of health and function is defined from the perspective of the individual and family and is concerned with the impact of disease on the physical, mental, social, and occupational functions of people's lives. Well-being is a much broader concept than health and function; it is the sense of life satisfaction of the individual, which is closer to the 1978 World Health Organization definition stated in chapter 2. The concept of well-being transcends health policy alone and becomes a major objective of all human activity.

Of these three possible alternative definitions of health, the population health perspective proposed here adopts the intermediate one of health and function as its basis, incorporating the expanded idea of maximizing function in a number of domains. Such a framework requires an operational measure of population health that goes beyond quantity of life (mortality) to add extra dimensions. In other words, the goal is to purchase not only life years but life years at some level of quality. In 1989, the government of Quebec stated its primary goals for "improving health and well-being" as "adding years to life, adding health to life, and adding well-being to life" (Quebec Ministry of Health

1989). Healthy People 2000, the current health goals for the United States, states an objective of "increasing years of healthy life to at least 65 in 2000" (USDHHS 1991).

An Aggregate Measure

How to measure health status has been of increasing concern to researchers and policymakers over the past several decades (Ware 1995; Patrick and Erickson 1993; Tarlov et al. 1989; Lohr 1990, 1992). Recently, it has been suggested that an appropriate aggregate measure of health and function might be health adjusted life expectancy (HALE), which combines the length and quality of life into an estimate of the number of years that can be expected in a specified state of health (Robine and Ritchie 1991; Robine 1993): an international organization fostering these concepts called the Network on Health Expectancy has been formed. Following this approach, measures like disability adjusted life years (DALYs), quality adjusted life years (QALYs), and years of healthy life (YHLs), discussed in the following sections, are specific ways of measuring the generic HALE concept.

If health adjusted life expectancy is to be the operational measurement of health and function, what does a population health framework add to this definition? Why is population health not simply the sum of the individual HALEs in the total population or subpopulation?

Beyond the Sum of Individual HALEs

From a narrow perspective, the sum of the health of individuals is, of course, equal to that of the population under consideration. However, this is too narrow a concept because it lulls us into thinking that improving health outcomes can be accomplished only by focusing on individual medical care interventions, which is still the dominant model operating today. Population health goes beyond public health or population based interventions to include all aspects of medical care that are effective in improving individual health and function. But a **population health** framework adds two additional considerations beyond the sum of individual health adjusted life expectancy. **The first is a broad understanding of the determinants of health or HALE.** Chapter 5 will present the evidence that in addition to the contributions made through medical care to individuals, progress in HALE also comes from improvements in socioeconomic status through increased levels of education and income and from preventive services at a group or population level (fluoridation, general health education), as well from investments in other sectors such as social services, genetics, and the environment.

While this does not change the definition of total population health adjusted life expectancy, it requires a broader perspective than simply providing medical care to individuals. Most of these nonmedical interventions, such as public health education and efforts to improve the environment, are introduced at the community or social level but have direct or indirect impact on the health of individuals; good examples for thinking about this are the reduction of harmful contaminants in air or water, reducing crime and violence, and public advertising campaigns regarding smoking or sexually transmitted diseases.

Balancing Resource Allocations

The second additional population health consideration is the economic or resource allocation perspective. If resources were not an issue, then any individual investment in medical care or other health determinants might be appropriate, even if it was very costly, was of questionable effectiveness, or was clearly ineffective but desired by the individual. But given that health care is financed to a considerable degree with public funds (46 percent, from table 4) and that employer and individual cash outlays are constrained as well, it is necessary to look at the most cost-effective means of getting value in terms of health outcomes. This will mean that expenditures on some individuals or on alternative determinants of health will have a much higher return than others in terms of the health adjusted life expectancy of the entire population.

Making such resource allocation decisions is difficult and has distributional considerations that will be discussed in chapters 6 and 8. However, it is naive to think that such allocation decisions are not being made now, some explicitly (all older persons are provided health insurance and many children are not) and some implicitly (many low-income areas have higher levels of environmental contamination). The population health perspective requires that purchasers, providers, and society consider the health of all individuals in addition to the health of particular individuals. This idea is summarized by the statement by Evans and Stoddart

> that a society that spends so much on health care that it cannot
> or will not spend adequately on other health enhancing ac-

tivities may actually be reducing the health of its population. (Evans and Stoddart 1990)

By this they mean that in a world where resources are limited, spending a large amount on one health determinant such as medical care, leaving fewer resources to invest in another area, such as the environment or education (with a possibly greater marginal return to health), could negatively affect the health not only of individuals but of the whole population.

Since Purchasing Population Health requires a quantifiable measure for financial incentives, for this purpose

population health is defined as the aggregate health outcome of health adjusted life expectancy (quantity and quality) of a group of individuals, in an economic framework that balances the relative marginal return from the multiple determinants of health.

Measuring Health Adjusted Life Expectancy (HALE)

Adopting a health adjusted life expectancy (HALE) framework for the definition of population health requires some concrete, operational measure of HALE that can be used for an accurate assessment of baseline health outcomes as well as any change from the baseline. Such a measure or measures must possess at least the following characteristics: scientific credibility from a theoretical perspective, unambiguous definition, availability of appropriate data, and validity for differentiating between various populations (Lillienfield and Stolley 1994; Patrick and Erickson 1993; McHorney 1994).

Measuring Mortality

Because other data sets or frameworks were not available, most early research dealt exclusively with indicators of length of life or mortality. While health related quality of life adjustments occupy much of the current research attention in this field, mortality remains a critical and perhaps the ultimate health outcome. There are several ways to measure life years or mortality using tools developed by demographers. Chapter 2 described some simple concepts, such as life expectancy at birth and age adjusted life expectancy. Now we will consider some of the other measures of mortality and their relative usefulness for the concept of Purchasing Population Health.

Crude Death Rate

The most basic measure is the crude death rate, expressed as deaths per 100,000 population. This statistic is available in most countries and is reported according to a standard set of international cause-of-death categories. The crude death rate is not usually used, since there are fundamental biologic differences in death rates by age and by gender (older persons and males die at higher crude death rates). Therefore, if one population has more old persons or more males, its crude death rate would "naturally" be higher than one with fewer such persons. The crude death rate would be correct but not useful for comparative purposes.

Age Adjusted Death Rates

To overcome the problem, the most widely used "corrected" mortality rate is age adjusted death rate, or standardized mortality rate (SMR), which was used for sex, race, and location in tables 1 and 2 in chapter 2. This standardization process essentially uses age-specific death rates for an entire population or a hypothetical standard one and creates a comparable age adjusted death rate for the two populations as if their age distributions were similar.

Because deaths are usually reported by cause, it is also useful to examine age adjusted cause-specific death rates in order to analyze the diseases responsible for different death rates. Table 5 shows changes in cause-specific death rates in the United States for selected categories from 1950 to 1990.

As the discussion in chapter 2 illustrated, overall death rates have declined from 841 to 520 (per 100,000) over the 40 years, with major decreases in deaths resulting from heart disease, cerebrovascular causes (strokes), and pneumonia/influenza. Rates from some specific causes such as lung cancer, homicide, and, of course, AIDS have increased, both absolutely and as a percentage of the lower total. The National Center for Health Statistics has recently published an atlas of U.S. mortality that shows the leading causes of death by race and sex for small geographic health service areas (Pickle et al. 1997).

Life Expectancy

Another way of measuring mortality is that of life expectancy, or the years of life remaining for a population or age group. This number is derived from demographic life tables and refers to the expected number of years persons reaching a certain age will live. This needs to be presented at least for each gender, given the biologic differences in death rates between males and females. In chapter 2 (table 3) this method was

TABLE 5. Cause-Specific Age Adjusted Death Rates, United States, 1950–1990

	1950	1990
All Causes	841/100,000	520/100,000
Heart disease	307 (37%)	152 (29%)
Cerebrovascular	89 (11%)	28 (5%)
Lung cancer	13 (2%)	41 (8%)
Colon cancer	19 (3%)	14 (3%)
Breast cancer	22 (3%)	23 (4%)
Pneumonia/influenza	26 (3%)	14 (3%)
Obstructive pulmonary disease	4 (0.5%)	20 (4%)
AIDS	0 (0%)	10 (2%)
Motor vehicle	23 (3%)	19 (4%)
Suicide	11 (1%)	12 (2%)
Homicide	4 (0.5%)	9 (2%)
Drug induced	—	4 (1%)
Alcohol induced	—	10 (2%)

Source: Data from USDHHS 1996.

used to show male and female life expectancy at birth for selected countries. The finding that the United States is doing better in international rankings with life expectancy at age 65 than at birth may provide some clues as to where the potential for improvements lies, since persons are likely to die of different causes at different ages. Similarly, life expectancy for males at 15 years of age, for example, would be independent of child mortality risks but would reflect the impact of motor vehicle accidents for that age group.

Infant Mortality

One common measure is infant mortality, which is defined not in relation to overall population but as the number of deaths under 1 year of age per 1,000 live births in the same year. This figure is widely cited as one major outcome indicator of national or regional health system performance.

Time Lost to Premature Death

For international comparisons, the World Bank has also used the concept of time lost to premature death, in which age adjusted death rates are compared to an international standard of achievement (World Bank 1993); others have occasionally made comparisons with what biologists might estimate maximum or ideal life expectancy to be. Sometimes

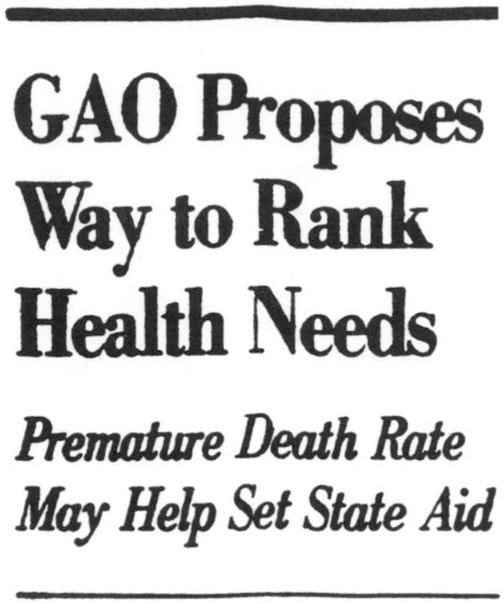

GAO Proposes Way to Rank Health Needs

Premature Death Rate May Help Set State Aid

FIG. 18.   Ranking state health needs.
(Copyright © 1997, the *Washington Post.*
Reprinted with permission.)

premature death rate estimates are reported as age adjusted death rates before age 65. In 1996 when Senator Nancy Kassebaum requested that the U.S. General Accounting Office identify the best way to determine the relative health needs of states, in order to have a way to allocate the funds in a new $1.1 billion public health block grant program, the premature mortality measure was identified as the "single best proxy for reflecting differences in the health status of states' populations" (U.S. General Accounting Office 1996; see fig. 18).

Table 6 shows data from such "years of potential life lost," in which any death under age 65 is arbitrarily considered to be premature. This table shows that different populations, in this case based on gender and ethnicity, have different levels of "premature" deaths. This varies by cause, of course. The largest difference is seen in homicide rates, while there is no difference between white and African American females in years of life lost as far as lung cancer is concerned.

Mortality Trends
In the United States, crude death rates have steadily declined from 9.5 per 1,000 in 1950 to 8.5 in 1991. Similarly, infant mortality in 1992 was at 8.5 per 100,000 live births, the lowest ever recorded; the 1950 rate was 29.2. In terms of life expectancy, increases at age 65 are now outpacing those at birth, a reversal of previous trends. Verbrugge has pointed out

TABLE 6.   Years of Potential Life Lost (U.S. 1990, before age 65, per 100,000 persons)

Cause	White Male	African American Male	White Female	African American Female
All deaths	6,503	14,364	3,331	7,382
Heart disease	838	1,398	310	782
Lung cancer	203	378	150	149
Breast cancer	—	—	218	264
AIDS	451	1,225	35	33
Homicide	313	2,581	98	510

Source: Data from USDHHS 1996.

that almost all mortality gains must now occur at older ages. Because of improvements in mortality rates in the young, a 20 year old could expect to live more than 24 of her next possible 25 years to age 45, while a 65-year-old man could expect 12.8 of the next 20 years (to age 85) and women aged 65 could expect 15.5 years (Verbrugge 1989). Using more recent data, Manton and colleagues cite 1993 census estimates that indicate that males age 65 can expect to live another 15.7 years and females age 65 for another 19.5 years (Manton, Stallard, and Corder 1995).

Clearly some measure of mortality needs to form the basis of a new outcomes purchasing standard, since there is no quality of life without life itself. Estimating the life expectancy of subpopulations, either by geographic location or by membership in a specific health plan, is complicated by changes in plan membership as well as by the uncertainty of future mortality rates for each age group, given the reductions that have already occurred over time. In addition, subpopulations may have additional biological or demographic characteristics that result in different distributions of life expectancy within the group. These heterogeneities clearly need to be recognized and dealt with when designing measurement standards for provider payment for Purchasing Population Health, and they are considered further in chapter 8. This is a complex but not impossible task, and we need to get started now (as Elliott Richardson says in the quote beginning this chapter) if we wish to get real value for our health care dollars.

Beyond Years of Life

Since 1970, work in this field has emphasized going beyond measures of mortality alone, again confirming the growing awareness that there is more to health than simply years of life. In addition, because mortality is a relatively infrequent event, it causes statistical measurement problems in small populations. Advances beyond mortality have been made possible through new methods for assessing the quality of life in specific disease states and for general health status. A considerable body of evidence has been accumulated regarding the validity and reliability of various approaches, drawing on concepts from psychology, sociology, economics, and operations research (Albrecht 1994).

Health status measurement experts Patrick and Bergner have categorized the domains of quality of life into relatively objective dimensions of "impairment," including symptoms, physical function, psychological function, and social function; the more subjective dimensions of "perceptions," including general health perceptions and satisfactions; and the domain of "opportunity," which includes concepts of disadvantage and resilience (Patrick and Bergner 1990). In addition, they make the point that most research has focused on "negative" aspects of health and therefore considers health improvement to be a reduction in illness or health related dysfunction and/or lengthening of life. They indicate that it is important to identify "positive" enhancements in relatively well individuals such as increased "energy, stamina, feeling of well-being, resilience, and productivity," even if longevity and morbidity are unaffected.

There is often definitional ambiguity about the concept of quality of life and the components or boundaries of morbidity and disability (Manton 1982). Verbrugge presents a model below (fig. 19) in which morbidity consists of disease incidence, duration, and severity, while disability is a subset of morbidity. People can exit from morbidity and disability by recovery, remission, or death; people can only move from disability to morbidity. This idea has also been shown by Manton in figure 20. These illustrative "survival curves" indicate the percentage of persons remaining alive, disabled, or reporting morbidity at each age. It can be seen, for example, that 60 years after birth about 88 percent are still alive, 80 percent are free of disability, and about 70 percent are without morbidity; each of these percentages gradually decreases at older ages.

Morbidity

Measuring morbidity is more difficult than measuring mortality and is only done on samples of the population. Morbidity data are generally concerned with the incidence and prevalence of specific medical condi-

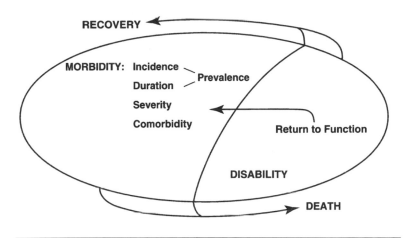

FIG. 19.   Morbidity and disability.
(From Verbrugge 1989. With permission from the *Annual Review of Public Health,* 10, copyright © 1989, by Annual Reviews Inc.)

tions in the population. At the national level, morbidity data is published by the National Center for Health Statistics (NCHS) and the Centers for Disease Control and Prevention (CDCP) (for reportable communicable diseases). NCHS morbidity sources include the Health and Nutrition Examination Survey, the Health Interview Survey, the Hospi-

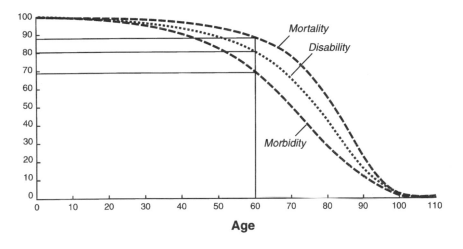

FIG. 20.   Morbidity, disability, and mortality.
(Adapted from Verbrugge 1989. With permission from the *Annual Review of Public Health,* 10, copyright © 1989, by Annual Reviews Inc.)

tal Discharge Survey, and the National Ambulatory Medical Care Survey. The results are published periodically in the *Vital and Health Statistics* and *Monthly Vital Statistics* reports and in the CDCP's *Morbidity and Mortality Weekly*. In addition, in the last decade NCHS has carried out a Health Promotion/Disease Prevention survey in order to monitor preventable conditions and preventive health behaviors.

There has recently been active discussion about the impact of increasing life expectancy on morbidity. In the 1980s, survey data from the previous decade revealed increasing numbers of chronic conditions and activity limitations among older persons (Verbrugge 1984), which were interpreted to reflect increased morbidity resulting from longer life and were termed the *failure of success*. Others reviewed these trends and suggested that the reported increases in morbidity might instead be due to changes in survey questions as well as better reporting practices (Wilson and Drury 1984; Gruenberg 1977). More recently, Manton and colleagues have presented evidence of significant declines in incidences of 16 medical conditions between 1982 and 1989 in persons over age 65 (Manton, Corder, and Stallard 1995; see table 7).

Overall, 11 of 16 conditions showed a decline over the period, with a significant 11 percent reduction in number of conditions per person. Similarly, Waidman and colleagues report on more recent improvements in self-reported limitations and chronic conditions in the 1980s; they suggest that the results from the 1970s were the result of early diagnosis of preexisting conditions in this period, as well as changes in individual reporting of limitation and disability, so that the evidence for declining morbidity was probably not accurate (Waidman, Bound, and Schoenbaum 1995).

Disability

Disability is a concept that is related to but not identical to morbidity. This is of more than semantic importance, because several previous measures of population health status combining mortality and morbidity have focused on disability alone as the morbidity component. The dictionary definition of disability refers to incapacity or inability. In health care this tends to be thought of in terms of conditions or illnesses that limit the ability to satisfactorily perform activities of daily living.

The Americans with Disabilities Act of 1990 defined disability as "a physical or mental impairment that substantially limits one or more of the major life activities." In the World Health Organization work described earlier, disability is linked both to the impact on individual performance and to the burden of disease; it does not, however, focus on

TABLE 7. Percent of Persons over Age 65 Reporting Symptoms of Selected
Chronic Conditions

Condition	1982	1989
Arthritis	68.8	63.1
Diabetes	11.0	12.4
Cancer	6.2	5.7
Hypertension	44.5	39.5
Stroke	3.4	2.6
Pneumonia	2.9	4.8
Broken hip/fractures	0.5	0.4
Mean number of conditions per person	2.5	2.3

Source: Data from Manton, Corder, and Stallard 1995.

the impact on social function. Verbrugge indicates that "disability is the
gap between the body's capability and the environment's demand"; she
also advocates including in this concept the two less common perspectives of unmet needs and loss of autonomy (Verbrugge 1989).

Statistical measures of disability have commonly included the
number of restricted activity and bed days and the number of persons
with long-term limitations of activity due to chronic illness. Since 1982,
the National Long Term Care Survey (NLTCS) has measured activities of
daily living (ADLs) and instrumental activities of daily living (IADLs);
the components of each measure are listed in table 8.

It has been recently reported that disability rates for the elderly
fell dramatically from 1989 to 1994, prompting speculation that future
Medicare expenditures for the elderly might not increase as dramatically as projected (Manton, Corder, and Stallard 1997).

Self-Reported Health Status

The range of morbidity measures available, as well as the substantial
issues of interpretation indicated in the preceding section, results in
much data but limited information, certainly for the purpose of measuring population health outcomes. Expecting that a single measure of
morbidity will accurately represent all morbidity is perhaps unrealistic.
In the past such measures have primarily focused on physical function
at the expense of social and mental function. This limitation has led
some to focus on the possibility of a single global measure of self-
reported health status, derived from the question, Would you say that
your health in general is excellent, very good, good, fair, or poor? This

TABLE 8.   Components of NLTCS Disability Measures

Inability to Perform without Assistance

ADL	IADL
1. Eating	1. Light housework
2. Getting in/out of bed	2. Laundry
3. Inside mobility	3. Meal preparation
4. Dressing	4. Grocery shopping
5. Bathing	5. Outside mobility
6. Toileting	6. Travel
	7. Money management
	8. Telephoning

Source: Data from Manton, Corder, and Stallard 1995.

has been asked in the National Health Interview Survey since 1972 and is a component of other indices or measurement tools.

As with other measures, the appropriateness of this question depends on its purpose, but it has been found to be a good predictor of mortality and hospitalization and has been utilized by several of the investigators discussed earlier regarding long-term trends in morbidity (Maddox and Douglass 1973; Weinberger et al. 1986). For example, Mossey and Shapiro, using Manitoba provincial survey and claims data, reported that the increased risk of death in the elderly who had poor self-rated health was greater than that associated with poor objective health status, poor life satisfaction, and low income; however, they did note that for one-third of the subjects, self-reported health failed to identify low objective health status (Mossey and Shapiro 1982). It is possible that such a general concept allows people to relate what other measures might miss, including incipient disease, disease severity, and physiologic-psychologic reserve, and perhaps to identify some of the aspects of positive health status discussed earlier by Patrick and Bergner. On the other hand, it is a subjective measure and may be imprecise and subject to manipulation.

Health Related Quality of Life

Another approach that goes beyond mortality is to consider quality of life directly. The term *quality* carries a definition of "relating to degree of excellence" and in the health status field is often used generically with regard to the excellence of life years. The boundary between health related quality of life and health and function is not crisp, but a generally accepted definition is that of "various aspects of a person's life which are strongly affected by changes in health status" and which "encompass dimensions such as generic and condition specific symptoms as well as physical, social, role, and sexual functioning, and mental health" (Cleary, Wilson, and Fowler 1994). This also has significant cultural considerations, discussed briefly in chapter 5.

Generic vs. Disease-Specific Measures

There is significant concern about the relative usefulness of individual disease-specific measures, in contrast to more generic summary measures of outcome. Many individual disease-specific measures are available; a few examples are shown in table 9.

Some argue that only multiple measures at a disease-specific level are appropriate (such as deaths from HIV or severity of depression), because only such specificity allows accurate measurement of health related quality of life. There is no question that such disease-specific measures are important and valuable for clinicians and programs working with specifically identified disease groups such as those with AIDS or mental illness or with patients with multiple chronic illnesses, either measuring improvements or lower rates of decline than are expected in many such diseases.

However, such disease-specific measures have limitations when one attempts to compare outcomes across different populations and different programs, since assessing the relative importance of improvement or decline in each measure is difficult if not impossible. For example, how should one value similar or dissimilar improvements in the Arthritis Impact Questionnaire and the Breast Cancer Index? Experts in this field have stated that a "preferred approach might be to use standardized instruments with disease-specific supplements"; such generic measures could then be used in parallel with specific measures where appropriate or necessary (Patrick and Deyo 1989).

Quality "Report Card" Indicators

As noted earlier, there has recently been increased interest in measures of quality of care, partly from an academic perspective but largely from the need to provide employers and individuals some standard of quality for health plans and managed care organizations to facilitate informed choices among them. Some of these measures have been developed by individual plans and for Medicare and Medicaid patients. More recently, the National Committee for Quality Assurance (NCQA) has

TABLE 9.   Selected List of Disease-Specific Measures

Diagnosis/Condition	Measure
Arthritis	McMaster-Toronto Arthritis Patient Reference Questionnaire (MACTAR)
	Health Assessment Questionnaire (HAQ)
	Functional Capacity Questionnaire
	American Rheumatism Association Classification
	Arthritis Impact Measurement Scales (AIMS)
Back pain	Disability Questionnaire
	Waddell Disability Index
	Oswestny Low Back Pain Disability Questionnaire
Cancer	Karnofsky Performance Status Measurement (KPS)
	Quality of Life Index (QLI)
	Functional Living Index: Cancer
	Breast Cancer
Chronic lung disease	Dyspnea Index
	Chronic Respiratory Disease Questionnaire

Source: Data from Patrick and Deyo 1989.

TABLE 10.   HEDIS 3.0 Effectiveness Measures

Reporting Set Measures

Advising smokers to quit (in Member Satisfaction Survey)
Beta blocker treatment after a heart attack
The health of seniors
Eye exams for people with diabetes
Flu shots for older adults
Cervical cancer screening
Breast cancer screening
Childhood immunization status
Adolescent immunization status
Treating children's ear infections
Prenatal care in the first trimester
Low–birth-weight babies
Checkups after delivery
Follow-up after hospitalization for mental illness

Source: Data from HEDIS/Report Cards 1997.

established a performance measurement program, the Health Plan Employer Data and Information Set (HEDIS), on which health plans voluntarily report and which purchasers are encouraged to use in judging plan quality (Iglehart 1996). The HEDIS system requires data on a variety of measures in the clinical arena as well as in the areas of access, patient satisfaction, and financial performance. Table 10 shows the measures in the "effectiveness" portion of the current HEDIS 3.0 "Reporting" Data Set (HEDIS/Report Cards 1997).

The data set also includes other measures in such areas as access, satisfaction, health plan stability, cost of care, "informed choices," and "descriptive" information. In addition, this new version also includes a set of "testing" measures that will be collected on an experimental or trial basis; examples are persons who smoke, depression treatment continuation, follow-up after Pap smear or mammogram, use of behavioral services, and health plan costs per member per month.

There is no question that such measures have a high degree of face validity and can be of great value for certain purposes; obviously, having higher immunization rates is better than having lower ones. It is also clear that program indicators such as eye care for diabetics are very important data in a diabetic clinic. But most of these measures do not meet the criteria for outcome measures presented earlier. Having high rates of Pap smears does not guarantee that they are read properly, that positive results are referred to treatment, that any indicated surgery is done promptly and with high quality, and that the net result is longer years of life at maximum levels of quality. Similarly, additional measures not shown such as high levels of customer satisfaction can be affected by factors that may be desirable, such as pleasant staff and facilities, but that do not necessarily mean that the patients will have longer and/or higher quality lives.

Much work by NCQA, FACCT, and other groups is being devoted to developing more sophisticated outcome components for report card measures like HEDIS. But so far these are not sufficient to determine if the overall goal of getting the most health for our health investments has been met. Epstein has recently concluded that such report card measures "can help identify health plans that are either outstanding or seriously substandard . . . but will never be comprehensive and will never be able to guarantee that important aspects of a health plan's quality of care have not deteriorated" (Epstein 1995). It is essential that we develop a better summary measure of length and quality of life for use in Purchasing Population Health, one that accurately reflects outcomes of large enrolled populations or communities and that can be used as a guide to investment at these levels.

A Single Measure:
The Gross National Health Product?

In terms of measuring and rewarding improvement in health adjusted life expectancy for an entire population, combining individual measures into an overall composite not only requires that many measures be collected and reported but also necessitates some weighing of each measure into the composite index. For example, how many years of life gained for patients with AIDS is equal to the reduction in depressive symptoms in other patients?

The advantage of a single aggregate measure or indicator is that it would allow accurate assessment of comparative baselines as well as changes across different populations. Having a common measure of benefit is essential when comparing alternative financial investments in a cost benefit framework. One of our most skilled and experienced public administrators, Elliott Richardson, says the following:

> At [the federal Department of] Health, Education, and Welfare, for example, we could have done a much better job in evaluating our programs if inputs of time, skill, and money had been reduced to a single quantum. This quantum, called a HEW, would have enabled us to make definitive comparisons of the results achieved by varying combinations of these inputs. A highly useful tool, wouldn't you agree? (Richardson 1996)

Similarly, Michael Wolfson from Statistics Canada makes a strong case for such a summary measure, which would be similar to other commonly used indicators like the gross domestic product and the Consumer Price Index (Wolfson 1994). He states that such a measure would initially be an object of policy interest, would focus attention on population health rather than on health care, and could be gradually incorporated into a financial incentive system. It is of interest that in 1979 Chen proposed such a single measure called the Gross National Health Product, but it and other suggestions of the time were too mathematically complex for common understanding and use (Chen 1976; Chen 1979; Sullivan 1971; Dean, West, and Weir 1982).

TABLE 11.   Examples of Aggregate HALE Measures

Name	Mortality Component	"Morbidity" Component
Quality adjusted life year (QALY)	Life expectancy	Quality adjustment factor from patients
Disability adjusted life year (DALY)	Life expectancy	50% decrease in six activity categories
Years of health life (YHL)	Life expectancy	One disability factor + self-reported health status

Moving toward Aggregate Measures

There have been significant developments since the Chen proposal, and there are now several potential approaches for a single measure of health adjusted life expectancy (HALE) that conform to the definition of population health identified at the beginning of this chapter and that allow the aggregate assessment of population morbidity and mortality together; as shown in table 11.

Quality Adjusted Life Years

The first method is that of the quality adjusted life year (QALY), which emphasizes the patient's valuation of health status as the quality modifier of life expectancy. Following early work in the United States and England (Weinstein and Stason 1977; Rosser and Kind 1978), this method was further elaborated by Torrance, who described the basic concept as "quite simple . . . utilities are cardinal values that are assigned to each health state on a scale that is established by assigning a value of 1.0 to being healthy and 0 to being dead. . . . the utility values reflect the quality of the health states and allow morbidity and mortality improvements to be combined into a single weighted measure, quality-adjusted life years (QALYs) gained" (Torrance 1986). Individual QALYs are calculated by multiplying the number of life years expected by the quality adjustment factor derived from patient valuation studies.

In the EuroQol rating scale, for example, patients are asked to value their own health state by choosing from three responses in each of five categories: mobility, self-care, usual activities, pain/discomfort, and anxiety/depression (Kind et al. 1994). This results in 243 possible combinations of health states, to which have been added unconsciousness and death. Individual valuations of these states are determined

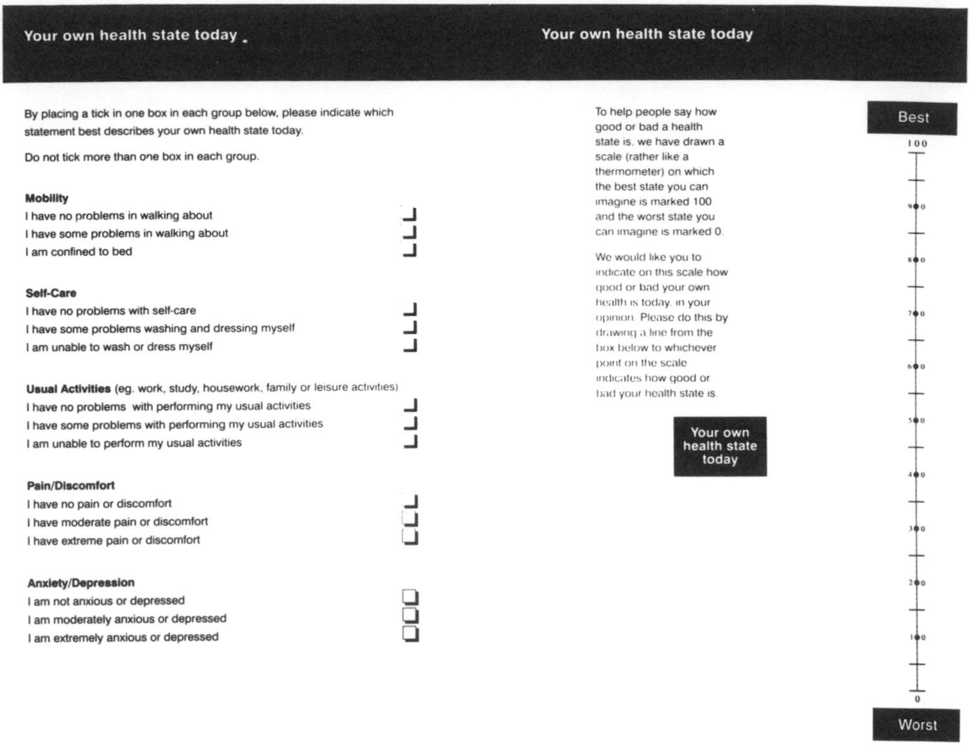

FIG. 21.   Measuring health adjusted life expectancy.
(From EuroQol Foundation.)

using a visual thermometer scale, where an individual places his or her own health state on a 0 to 100 scale from "worst imaginable" to "best imaginable," shown in figure 21.

The patient's own valuations can then be used to make adjustments of expected life years in different states for alternative treatments or programs, such as seen in figure 22 for medical management vs. surgery in patients with severe angina and left main vessel coronary artery disease (Williams 1986).

This data shows that in profile B with medical management, quality of life declines slightly for three years and much more rapidly in year four, with expected death on average in year five. With surgery in this class of patients, life years are extended for another six years but with reduced quality of life from years five to eleven. Much of the QALY work has been used in application to different treatments and preventive approaches. When combined with cost data, this work results in

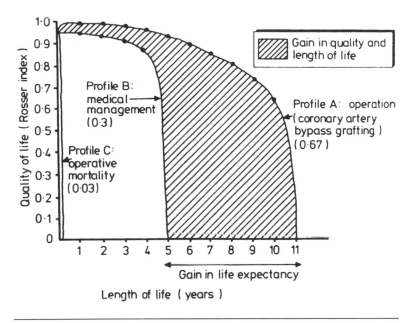

FIG. 22. Quality and length of life in heart disease.
(From Williams 1986, *British Medical Journal* 291:327.)

QALY "league tables" that compare the cost for the number of QALYs gained from different interventions. These are covered in more detail in chapter 6 and table 14. Most of the work has focused on the individual patient level, but Williams has begun to utilize this data in analyzing the equity of distribution of health status across populations (Williams 1996, 1997b).

Disability Adjusted Life Years

A second aggregate measure under active development is that of disability adjusted life years (DALY). Much initial work focused on the combination of mortality and disability, primarily because of the existence and increased quality of survey data of disability measures. As indicated in figures 19 and 20, disability is related to morbidity and refers specifically to reduced function in a variety of domains.

An early example of this approach was that of Katz and colleagues (Katz et al. 1983), who used activity of daily living data from a sample of noninstitutionalized people in Massachusetts to determine a measure of active life expectancy. More recently, Murray has reported on the development of the DALY as a new indicator of the burden of

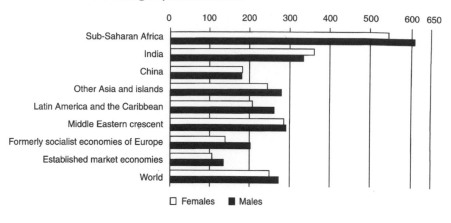

FIG. 23.   Disease burden for selected countries.
(From World Bank, *World Development Report 1993: Investing in Health* [New York: Oxford University Press, 1993], 28.)

disease, which uses experts to provide relative weights for a 50 percent reduction in six classes of activity limitation (similar to those in table 8) (Murray 1994). A generic concern about disability approaches is that they appear to be "burden of disease" influenced and do not take into account morbidity that does not lead to serious loss of physical function or that occurs outside the physiologic or medical model realm. For example, the DALYs proposed by Murray require more than 50 percent reduction in function to be counted. On the other hand, they are constructed in large part using data that exists or is being collected in a growing number of population health surveys. This measurement is being used most extensively by the World Bank for cross-national comparison and has been claimed by Foege to "have the potential to revolutionize the way in which we measure the impact of disease" (Foege 1994). Figure 23 shows some of the cross-national results obtained by the World Bank.

Years of Healthy Life

A third approach is that of years of healthy life (YHL) from Erickson and colleagues in the United States. This measure combines two questions already asked in the National Health Interview Survey, one from the disability activity limitation category as well as one regarding general perception of health. This second addition takes the YHL measure beyond the more narrow disability only (DALY) approach critiqued previously. These two questions create a matrix of 30 combinations, to

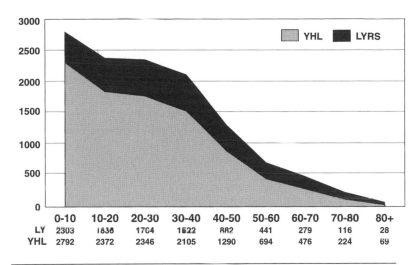

	0-10	10-20	20-30	30-40	40-50	50-60	60-70	70-80	80+
LY	2303	1838	1704	1522	882	441	279	116	28
YHL	2792	2372	2346	2105	1290	694	476	224	69

FIG. 24. Health adjusted life expectancy: life years vs. years of healthy life, 1990 U.S.
(Data from Erickson et al. 1995, NCHS Health People Statistical Notes #7, USPHS.)

which utility values are assigned that range from 1.00 for persons without role limitation and in excellent health to 0.10 for persons limited in function and in poor health. These valuations are then applied to age cohorts to create a combination HALE that the researchers call years of healthy life (Erickson, Wilson, and Shannon 1995). The advantage of this measure is that it combines disability data with self-reported health status, creating a measure that is available from survey data and represents individual value, but it does so by extrapolating from existing data without doing individual patient surveys as in the EuroQol approach.

Figure 24 is a graphical way to illustrate the YHL approach to population health outcome measurement. The black area represents all of the future life years (LY) of the 1990 U.S. population. It is determined by multiplying the number of persons in the United States in each age interval by the average number of years of life remaining for someone in that interval; when these are summed across the age intervals, the total future life years of the population equal about 12,400 million. This assumes, of course, that future death rates in each age cohort are the same as in 1990.

As indicated earlier, mortality alone is an incomplete measure of health outcome. When these life years are multiplied by a morbidity or quality adjustment factor for each age interval (in this method a combination of disability level and self-reported health status), the result is years of healthy life, represented by the gray area. This measure produces a total of about 9,000 million YHLs, about 27 percent less than life years (LYs). There is relatively more space at the higher age end of the curve between life years and years of healthy life, representing increased activity limitations and diminished perceived health status at the older end of the age distribution.

I believe a compelling case can be made for such an aggregate measure of health outcome to guide purchasing considerations for moderate to large managed care plans and communities. This does not exclude the usefulness of additional disease-specific measures for individual clinical settings and programs and for process measures like HEDIS to identify priority areas for improvement. However, without such a broad and relatively simple measure of health outcome it will be impossible to compare fairly the wide variety of plans and systems for macro financing purposes. The only alternative would be a massive index of hundreds of smaller outcome and process components, with agreed upon weights for each component of the index. This would be a very complicated analytic task and even if possible would be difficult to explain. With health adjusted life expectancy adopted as the conceptual measure of health outcome for the purpose of Purchasing Population Health, it is both possible and advantageous to quickly but carefully move to an aggregate measure such as years of healthy life as the specific measurement tool for a health outcome incentive standard.

The Tyranny of Outcomes?

A leading thinker and advocate of health care quality improvement, Donald Berwick, has ascribed the lack of practical evolution of outcome measurement and quality assurance partly to the "tyranny of outcomes," which a Purchasing Population Health framework might encourage (Berwick 1988). He cautions that the efficacy of many health care practices is unknown, that one-dimensional measurement strategies may miss underlying multiple and independent attributes of health, that process characteristics such as respect and caring have value, and that evaluation can detect flaws in design or process even if a defective product has not yet been produced "downstream." Smith in England has described a series of "unintended consequences" of managing to performance indicators (such as tunnel vision, less than optimal performance, and gaming) and suggests strategies for dealing with them (Smith 1995). Similarly, Heather Palmer has indicated that issues such as patient preferences, unknown risk factors, sample size, time for outcomes to be observed, and error in patient reported outcomes pose difficulties for outcome measurements; she indicates her preference for disease-specific guideline performance measures (Palmer 1995).

It is legitimate to ask whether process measures such as satisfaction or provider compassion or quality of facilities should be given weight in a Purchasing Population Health framework. It cannot be denied that these are important considerations to almost everyone and in addition have economic value. It might be useful to separate such process components measures into three categories with regard to their impact on health outcomes.

First, some process factors such as peace of mind or compliance with medication routine, which actually contribute to the healing process, are at least theoretically incorporated into this framework, since positive outcomes will be increased. In the second category it is likely that there are some aspects of care that may actually reduce positive outcomes, such as the charming but unqualified surgeon or procedures that are harmful (such as using unnecessarily powerful or inappropriate drugs that cause disease themselves). Even if such things are desired by patients, there is no rationale for encouraging them, and they probably should be eliminated through whatever mechanism is effective.

This leaves us with the third intermediate category of process components that may be desired by patients or providers but neither help nor hurt outcome (amenities such as wine in the hospital, private rooms, art in the clinics, staff friendliness, etc.). How these should be valued is less clear, although I must express a bias that they ought to be judged luxuries, available to those who want to use their own resources to acquire them. Some persons consider them very important: a recent study revealed that a significant fraction of patients in a Scottish infertility clinic would have preferred not to become pregnant (a fairly clear outcome indicator) if staff attitudes were not satisfactory (Ryan 1996). My current view is that public resources (and I would argue employer-sponsored insurance as well) should not be used for such "beyond outcome" investments while measurable outcome improvement is still possible for other patients. It is also possible in a competitive system that such issues will be dealt with in part through patient choice of health plans. Issues of economic distribution of scarce resources will be dealt with more fully in chapter 6.

Such concerns and process considerations must be accommodated in a Purchasing Population Health framework. But in the absence of an ultimate outcome standard such as health adjusted life expectancy, a tyranny of process can and does become an end in itself. More than a few organizations have invested much time and resources in managerial processes such as corporate restructuring and/or quality improvement, with little demonstrated benefit to patients in terms of ultimate health outcomes.

There is still much uncertainty regarding what is effective in producing population health, and this is likely to continue for some time, if not forever. For those interventions that are relatively clear, professional guidelines such as those advocated by Palmer will be adopted by organizations at the patient care level and built into professional practice and reward structures. But for many less certain interventions, a global incentive at the integrated organizational level will encourage professional and administrative creativity to identify additional interventions that are most cost effective in producing the desired outcome for the whole population.

As opposed to our being continually locked into incentives that reward only for providing additional medical services and increased revenues, the HALE Purchasing Population Health outcome framework will lead to scores of natural efforts and experiments to find medical and health interventions that will produce units of outcome improvement at the lowest marginal cost. As these become proven in terms of cost-effectiveness, they will be incorporated into standard practices, while incentives for improvement will continue to encourage a marketplace of innovation.

Imagine how different it would be if our doctors and hospitals were responding to organizational imperatives to produce healthier populations! Almost certainly, such motivation and incentives would return us to the patient advocacy values embodied by the nineteenth century general practitioner, but in a twenty-first century technical and financial reality.

Summary

This chapter has described current measures of health outcome and quality and argued that a single aggregate measure such as health adjusted life expectancy would be most appropriate for the financial incentives that Purchasing Population Health envisions. So far, this has been discussed at a total population level; issues involving individual health plans and community heterogeneity will be considered in chapter 8, Different Populations, Different Needs? But first, in chapter 5 we will examine the multiple determinants that produce health outcomes, so that an appropriate and balanced investment strategy can be devised.

5 · The Multiple Determinants of Health

How much, then, should go for medical care, and how much
for other programs affecting health, such as pollution control,
fluoridation of water, accident prevention, and the like? There
is no simple answer, partly because the question has rarely
been explicitly asked.
   —Victor Fuchs, 1974

A society that spends so much on health care that it cannot or
will not spend adequately on other health enhancing activities
may actually be reducing the health of its population.
   —Robert Evans and Greg Stoddart, 1990

So far we have demonstrated that the goal of obtaining maximum health
from our investments has not yet been fully achieved. We have made a
case for using health adjusted life expectancy (HALE) as the outcome
standard for public and private purchasers. But how will improvements
in HALE be made? How will a purchaser or a society know what the
most cost-effective investment strategy is? This chapter focuses on what
is known about how population health is produced and improved; only
by understanding this process and its components can an appropriate
investment strategy for Purchasing Population Health be determined.
This chapter is organized into nine sections, each of which describes
how a particular determinant affects health status:

   · The Role of Medical Care
   · An Expanded Model for the Determinants of Health
   · Socioeconomic Determinants
   · How Social Determinants Affect Individual Biology
   · The Role of Heredity
   · Environment: The World around Us
   · Is Health an Individual Responsibility?
   · The Role of Public Health
   · Short Term vs. Long Term

The Role of Medical Care

The starting point for thinking about the determinants of health is with
medical care, the diagnostic and therapeutic interventions in disease

processes that attempt to allay symptoms, restore function, and extend length and quality of life. The scientific developments in medicine are one of the wonders of the twentieth century, with advances in diagnostic technology, surgery, and pharmaceuticals that no one would have predicted several decades ago. New treatments for cancer and for heart disease have contributed to the quantifiable increased life expectancy we now enjoy and have been described in previous chapters. Other examples of clinical interventions of great benefit are hip replacements that provide improved quality of life in elderly patients and the chemical treatment of depression. Additional progress is expected in the future from advances in new pharmaceuticals, genetic engineering, noninvasive therapies, and behavioral medicine.

Given the widespread understanding and acceptance of the role of medical care in altering disease processes, it is not necessary to summarize all the evidence of medical progress in the last century. In one recent article, written in part as a response to the evidence that other nonmedical factors have contributed to improvements in health, John Bunker and his colleagues highlight the role of clinical preventive services, such as screening for hypertension and cervical cancer and immunizations for many infectious diseases, and estimate that they have led to about one and one-half years of additional life expectancy, with the potential for an additional seven or eight months if fully utilized by persons at risk (Bunker, Frazier, and Mosteller 1994; Bunker 1995). In addition, treatments for conditions such as cancer of the cervix and colon, heart disease, hypertension, diabetes, pneumonia, and influenza are estimated to have added three to four and one-half years to life expectancy, with the potential for another one and one-half years from full application of existing technologies.

Other investigators, primarily from a public health perspective, have challenged the extent to which medical care has been responsible for the gains in life expectancy in the last century. McKeown has provided historic evidence that declines in mortality preceded the development of modern therapies, with graphs as in figure 5, showing the decline of tuberculosis mortality before prevention and treatment, and figure 25, indicating improvements in mortality preceding the rapid growth in medical expenditures (McKeown 1976).

These gains are attributed to general improvements in nutrition, sanitation, and water supplies that accompanied the socioeconomic development of this period. This in part explains the transition from infectious diseases as the major contributor to mortality in the early

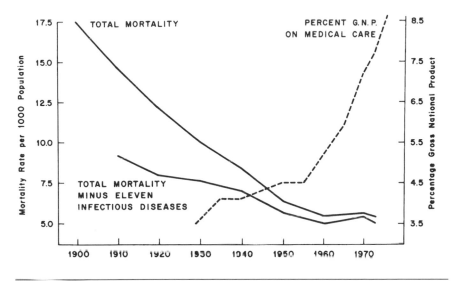

FIG. 25.   U.S. mortality rates and health expenditure.
(From *Milbank Quarterly* Summer, 1977, 55 [3]: 415.)

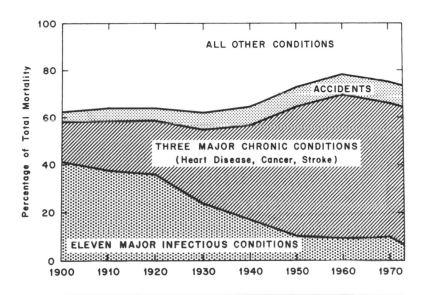

FIG. 26.   Contribution of chronic and infectious conditions to mortality, U.S.
(From *Milbank Quarterly* Summer, 1977, 55 [3]: 416.)

decades of this century to chronic diseases associated with longer life expectancy, as illustrated in figure 26.

McKinlay and colleagues challenge Bunker's perspective and assert that medical measures are responsible for only 3.5 percent of the decline in infectious disease mortality in the United States since 1900. They also examine the major chronic disease killers such as coronary heart disease and cancer. For coronary heart disease, they discuss the scientific evidence for the effects of lowering blood pressure and cholesterol, emergency medical services and coronary care units, by-pass surgery, and beta blocking agents in the post–myocardial-infarction patient. While most of these medical interventions have some impact, McKinlay argues that the impact on overall mortality is small, in large part because the measures that are effective impact on a very small number of persons in the overall population (such as those surviving myocardial infarction) (McKinlay, McKinlay, and Beaglehole 1989).

The point to be taken from this debate is not that one argument is right and the other wrong, for this is certainly not the case. As will be shown in the next section, both medical care and other determinants of health have a role to play in producing improvements in mortality and morbidity.

> **The challenge now in Purchasing Population Health, in an era of limited resources, is to move toward that optimal balance of resource allocation across the known determinants of health that will produce the greatest improvement for the most people with the resources available.**

While this is a significant challenge, it is within the range of possibility and will be covered in more depth in chapters 6 and 9.

An Expanded Model for the Determinants of Health

Many discussions of the determinants of health have difficulty avoiding a tone that is critical of medical care; this understandably offends health professionals and confuses patients who have benefited from medical care. It often appears that one has to take one side or the other: that of total reliance on and respect for medical care or, alternatively, questioning the value of any scientific or medical intervention. It is not clear why this polarization has taken place; perhaps it came to popular attention with the 1976 publication of *Medical Nemesis: The Expropriation of Health,* by Ivan Illich, which questioned the value of most of medicine and medical care (Illich 1976).

In academia such polarization is often related to competition or disagreement between disciplines, with criticism of science and medicine often coming from economics, sociology, or nonmedical health professions. It would be hard to discount the financial and professional power of physicians and the medical industry, which provides a target for these criticisms. As both a health policy researcher and a physician, I want to make it very clear that I value the contributions that medical care makes and will continue to make to my health, to the health of my family, and to all people with access to it.

In fact, it is undoubtedly the wonders of modern medicine that are responsible for the dominant public view that medical care is the only or the predominant contributor to health. The parallel truth is that there is a less well recognized but large and growing body of evidence supporting the independent contributions of factors other than medical care in the health of populations.

The Population Health Group of the Canadian Institute for Advanced Research has recently been responsible for pulling together much of this information in the previously cited book *Why Are Some People Healthy and Others Not?* and in an issue of *Daedalus* called "Health and Wealth" (Evans, Barer, and Marmor 1994; *Daedalus* 1994). In these publications, Professor Robert Evans and his colleagues have called attention to two alternative ways of viewing the production of health. We have previously seen their illustration (fig. 2) of the more narrow but commonly held view in which health care is said to be analogous to a heating system. People become sick for a variety of unspecified reasons and present themselves to the health care system for care and cure. The health care system is both a thermostat and furnace, with the response to colder temperatures (more disease) being to turn up the heat (more health care).

In this view of the world, health policy is identical to health (medical) care policy, with no other factors or determinants recognized. Evans and Stoddart's more complete model was also briefly introduced in chapter 2 (fig. 3). It is reproduced here (fig. 27) to focus attention on the broad range of factors that impacts on health outcomes.

Recall that disease is distinct from both health and function as well as from well-being. Disease is the dysfunction identified and

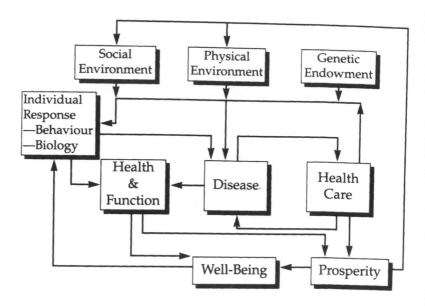

FIG. 27.   Multiple determinants of health model.
(Reprinted with permission from Evans, Robert G., et al. [eds.] *Why Are Some People Healthy and Others Not? The Determinants of Health of Populations* [New York: Aldine de Gruyter] Copyright © 1994, Walter de Gruyter Inc., New York.)

treated by the medical care system, while the concept of health and function explains the manner in which symptoms and conditions are experienced by the individual. The concept of well-being is a higher order function, that of total life satisfaction, which is broader than that of health and function.

The figure indicates that in addition to health care, other factors impact on both disease and health and on function. It identifies the broad categories of genetic endowment, the physical environment, and the social environment as not only influencing disease but also as playing a role in the individual response to both disease and to health and function.

The balance of this chapter will develop the evidence supporting this broad view of the production of health and will describe what is known about the importance of each factor. In addition, possible biologic mechanisms for how social determinants produce disease or dysfunction will be addressed.

Socioeconomic Determinants

The Socioeconomic Gradient: More Wealth, Better Health?

The most compelling evidence for the role of nonmedical factors in population health (beyond the "negative" historic evidence preceding) is the persistent finding that higher levels of socioeconomic status are directly associated with lower levels of mortality and morbidity.

This has been termed the *socioeconomic gradient* in health status (Adler et al. 1993; Adler et al. 1994). Socioeconomic status is a concept that generally includes such factors as education, income, and social/occupational class; these are obviously interrelated factors, and care must be taken when attempting to explain their independent impact on health.

The most important work in understanding this relationship is that of the British social epidemiologist Michael Marmot and his colleagues. Their initial findings came from a unique data set called the Whitehall Survey, which followed more than 10,000 British civil servants over more than two decades. These middle-aged male employees were grouped into four occupational classifications according to hierarchy and status: administrative, professional-executive, clerical, and other. The striking initial findings were that age adjusted mortality rates were three and one-half times higher in the lowest status manual grade than in the highest administrative grade and that there was a gradient in mortality from the lowest to the highest (Marmot, Kogevinas, and Elston 1987; Marmot and Davey-Smith 1989; Marmot 1994). This gradient was evident for many causes of death, as illustrated in figure 28.

Very striking is the finding that the mortality gradient still remained when traditional risk factors were taken into account. This is demonstrated in figure 29, which shows how the relative risk of coronary heart disease increased from 1.0 to 4.0 as job status decreased. It also shows that lower status employees have higher levels of risk factors such as smoking, high blood pressure, and high cholesterol but that most of the differences in mortality are unexplained by these risk factors. In addition, historical data in England show that a similar gradient has persisted over most of the years since 1911 when the data were first collected. It is important to note that all of these persons were employed in government civil service jobs, and so these differences cannot be explained by poverty or extreme deprivation. Recent evi-

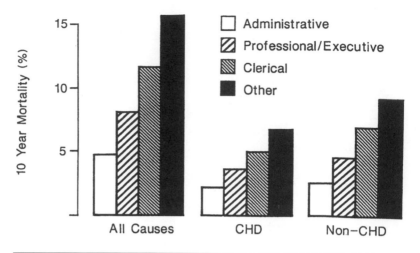

FIG. 28. 10 year mortality by occupation.
(From "Social Differentials in Health Within and Between Populations"
reprinted by permission of *Daedalus: Journal of the American Academy of
Arts and Sciences,* from the issue entitled, "Health and Wealth," Fall 1994,
Vol. 123, No. 4.)

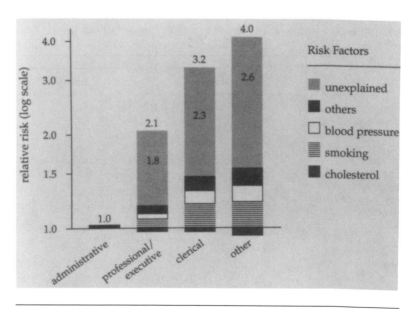

FIG. 29. Coronary heart disease, occupation, and risk factors.
(From Marmot et al. 1978, Courtesy of BMJ Publishing Group.)

dence is beginning to shed light on which aspects of occupational hierarchy are related to the risk of mortality, with level of control over job function emerging as important (Bosma, Marmot, Hemingway et al. 1997).

The British civil service studies cited in the preceding demonstrate a relationship between health and employment hierarchy or status. Similar evidence has been put forth in the United States and elsewhere for both mortality and morbidity. Because rigid employment classifications such as those examined in Britain were not available, these studies have relied on other measures of socioeconomic status such as income and education. The biological mechanisms that could be responsible for the association of such factors with increased disease and death will be discussed later. First, however, we will examine the evidence about the impact of individual components of the socioeconomic environment on health status.

Better Educated and Healthier?

Level of education has been associated with health status and mortality for some time, particularly in developing countries. The relationship between maternal literacy and child mortality has been clearly established. Initially this was thought to operate through the increased economic status that greater literacy brings, but recent studies have isolated the independent effect of literacy and schooling from income levels. A 1985 United Nations study of 15 developing countries indicated that the effect of an additional year of mother's schooling resulted in a 3.4 percent reduction in mortality; this impact was greater than the sum of doubling income, piped water, and toilets as well as moving from agricultural to white collar work (Grosse and Auffrey 1989).

In the United States, in 1973 Kitagawa and Hauser demonstrated a graded relationship between education and mortality, with significantly lower levels of mortality in 1960 for those with college education than for those with less than high school levels (Kitagawa and Hauser 1973). Similar findings have also been reported for morbidity, such as chronic disease, hypertension, and cervical cancer.

A very important recent study in the United States by Pappas and his colleagues reanalyzed the data of Kitagawa and Hauser from 1960 and extended it to 1986 (Pappas et al. 1993). They showed that mortality rates were lower but that decreases in mortality were greatest in the more educated groups.

This indicates not only that the gradient persists but that the inequality in mortality in relation to educational level has increased in each subgroup of the population over the 26 years studied; for African American and white men it doubled, and it grew 30 percent for African American women and 23 percent for white women.

Another study, by Guralnik and colleagues, compared whites and African Americans in 1987 in the North Carolina Piedmont area with regard to active life expectancy (mortality plus disability). Mortality differences between older African Americans and whites were eliminated when adjusting for educational level between the racial groups; higher educational attainment was related to a marked advantage in all race-gender subgroups. The increase ranged from 2.5 to 4.6 years of life expectancy and from 2.4 to 3.9 years of active (disability-free) life expectancy (Guralnik et al. 1993). The authors of this study conclude that "increasing the likelihood that a person will attain a high level of education not only may be advantageous for that person's young and middle years as a wage earner but also may be a valuable investment in increasing his or her years of active, nondisabled life after retirement." These findings must also raise our sensitivity to the meaning of a socioeconomic characteristic such as race; in many cases it is easier to measure representations (skin color) than the more complex underlying components associated with such a factor.

The association of higher education level with longer and healthier life does not explain the mechanism for the relationship. Speculation has centered on the impact that knowledge has on productivity and income, on more appropriate utilization of health services, on healthier lifestyles (e.g., with regard to alcohol consumption, smoking, driving), and on community cohesion. Smoking behavior partially explains the impact of education on mortality for middle-aged and older persons and was found to be primarily responsible for the impact of educational levels on low-birth-weight babies (Feldman et al. 1989; Kleinman and Madans 1985). The distinguished economist Victor Fuchs has observed that education helps individuals make better use of available medical care resources, as well as helping them better appreciate the importance of making current health investments (i.e., stopping smoking) for future benefit (Fuchs 1983). In summary, whatever its mechanism, there is a strong case for the importance of educational attainment as one component of the socioeconomic gradient.

Higher Income, Better Health?

It is not surprising to think that there might be a relationship between income and health status. Many studies, particularly of developing countries, have shown such results, especially at the low end of the income scale. Figure 15 demonstrated the relationship between life expectancy and GDP per capita for 1990 for a number of developing countries. The impact is strong at the bottom of the curve, probably due both to general socioeconomic factors such as nutrition, housing, and water and to medical care.

Such striking relationships are not found in developed countries, where there are diminishing returns to health as per capita income increases. Richard Wilkinson, from Sussex, England, has studied the 23 member countries of the Organization for Economic Cooperation and Development (OECD) (Wilkinson 1992a,b). He found a low correlation between life expectancy and GDP per capita in 1986–87 and no correlation looking at changes in life expectancy and per capita GDP increase between 1970 and 1990 (fig. 30). A possible interpretation for this is that all of these countries are at the "flat of the curve" as illustrated in figure 15, so that no relationship would necessarily be expected.

But Wilkinson went further, following up on previous studies that suggested that it was not the absolute level of income but the equality of distribution of income in a society that showed this relationship, particularly at the high end of the income curve. Comparable data on income distribution is difficult to find, but figures of good comparability exist for nine developed countries from the Luxembourg Income Study (Wilkinson 1994). Figure 31 shows the strong positive relationship between life expectancy at birth and the percentage of income received by the bottom 70 percent of families.

With another data set Wilkinson also showed a similar significant, negative relationship between change in life expectancy and change of the proportion of persons in poverty between 1975 and 1985 (fig. 32). He also points out that Japan currently has both the highest level of life expectancy (which cannot be explained by diet or availability of health services) and the most egalitarian income distribution.

The income effect is not just between rich and poor but between different levels of socioeconomic status. Wilkinson discards explanations of greater medical care or reverse causality in which sicker persons are poorer through lower wages. He suggests that the effect is less related to the physical effects of lower income than to the psychoso-

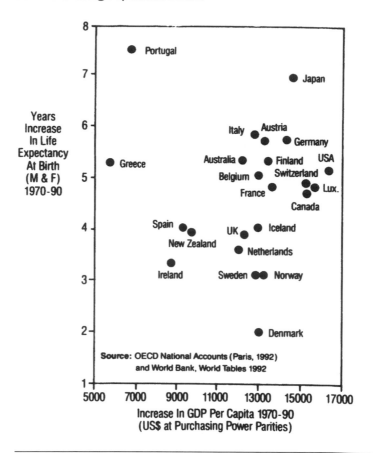

FIG. 30. Increase in GDP per capita vs. increase in life expectancy.
(From "The Epidemiology Transition: From Material Scarcity to Social
Disadvantage" reprinted by permission of *Daedalus: Journal of the American
Academy of Arts and Sciences,* from the issue entitled, "Health and Wealth,"
Fall 1994, Vol. 123, No. 4.)

cial meanings of such disadvantage and deprivation in a given society or
community. An active debate over these findings continues in the *British Medical Journal* (Judge 1995; Wilkinson 1995).

In the United States, the impact of income inequality on mortality was examined in the same Pappas 1960–86 study discussed previously with regard to education. Similarly, it was found that the impact of income inequality was even greater than that from educational inequality, with doubling of mortality levels among unrelated persons and tripling among family members. As indicated in the preceding, the

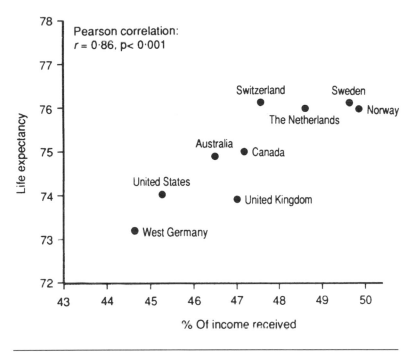

FIG. 31. Percentage of income received by the lowest 70 percent vs. life expectancy.
(*British Medical Journal,* 1992, 304:166.)

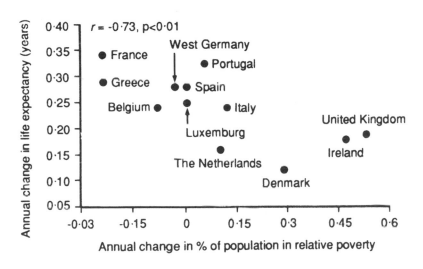

FIG. 32. Annual rate of change in life expectancy and proportion in poverty.
(*British Medical Journal,* 1992, 304:166.)

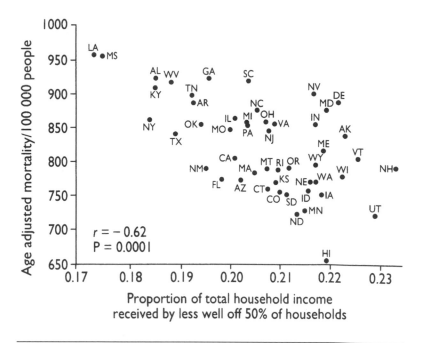

FIG. 33.   Income distribution and mortality, U.S. states, 1990.
(From Kaplan et al. 1996, *British Medical Journal,* 1996, 312:1000.)

impacts of income and education certainly have interrelationships that need to be considered.

An additional recent study demonstrates the income inequality association in the United States. Kaplan and colleagues examined the relationship between age adjusted mortality across the 50 states and the proportion of income received by the poorer 50 percent of the population in each state (Kaplan et al. 1996). Figure 33 shows the strong negative relationship between these two variables.

This was unaffected by adjusting for state median incomes, confirming the Wilkinson hypothesis. Significant correlations were also found with rates of homicide and violent crime and with the percentage of low-birth-weight babies in a state.

In a rare social experiment in Gary, Indiana, from 1971 to 1974, a negative income tax increased incomes to the poverty level for half of 1,799 eligible families. Results indicated an increase in birth weight of 0.3 to 1.2 pounds in the income supplemented group, thought primarily to be caused by increased maternal nutrition (Kehrer and Wolin 1979).

There are also indications that other socioeconomic factors, probably closely related to income, are responsible for poorer health. Primarily in the British literature, factors such as number of elderly persons living alone, the unemployment rate, and the proportion of dependents in single career households have been found to be independently associated with higher mortality rates (Davey Smith, Bartley, and Blane 1990).

You Can't Do It Alone

Associations between social relationships and health status have been noted for decades (Berkman 1984). Early studies documented relationships between lack of social integration and suicide, tuberculosis, accidents, and schizophrenia; in addition, married persons have lower age adjusted mortality rates from all causes than unmarried persons. In these early studies, however, it was not clear if poor health caused the poor relationships or vice versa.

The 1970s saw a great expansion of research in this field, driven by interest in stress and psychosocial relationships in death and disease. In 1979, Berkman and Syme reported on a prospective survey in Alameda County, California, that overcame some of the limitations of previous research. They examined the impact on mortality of a "social network" index comprised of four factors: marriage, contacts with family and friends, church membership, and other formal and informal group affiliations (Berkman and Syme 1979). They found that persons low on the index were twice as likely to die as those high on the index, after controlling for other factors such as physical health, socioeconomic status, smoking, alcohol consumption, obesity, and use of preventive services, as shown in figure 34.

Using more precise methods, other investigators in the United States and elsewhere have found similar results. James House, chair of the Sociology Department at the University of Michigan, with his colleagues has summarized the results of several of these studies in figure 35. He argues that the results of such studies demonstrate a stronger relationship between social support and mortality than the link between mortality and cigarette smoking or the correlation beween personality type and coronary heart disease (House, Landis, and Umberson 1988).

Such studies have also been extended to determine whether social support has its primary impact on reducing the onset or progression of disease or survival after an event. Lisa Berkman has summarized the results of five studies looking at the influence of social ties following

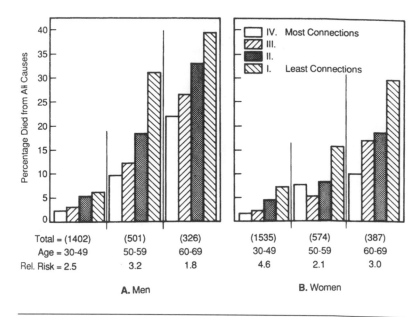

FIG. 34.   Mortality rates and social networks.
(From L. Berkman and S. Syme, 1979, "Social Networks, Host Resistance, and
Mortality: A Nine-Year Follow-up Study of Alamada County Residents"
American Journal of Epidemiology 109: 190.)

a heart attack. In her own work, she found that six months after
discharge, 53 percent of patients with no social support had died, compared with 36 percent with one source of social support and 23 percent
with two or more, after controlling for factors such as clinical severity,
age, socioeconomic status, and depressive symptoms (Berkman 1995).

There is also some interesting evidence regarding individual
reactions to racism in terms of health status. Dressler has examined the
reasons for higher levels of hypertension in African Americans and
finds that darker skin color is associated with higher blood pressure
levels, independent of socioeconomic variables (Dressler 1991). He and
others provide beginning evidence that suggests that frustrating social
interactions and color-based barriers, including greater unemployment,
family instability, and criminal victimization, can produce stress that
has other pathophysiologic effects such as poor pregnancy outcomes,
diabetes, and even cancer and heart disease. There are racial differences
in mortality and use of services among Medicare beneficiaries (Gornick
et al. 1996). Feagin has observed that many African Americans experience more than isolated incidents of discrimination, including repeated

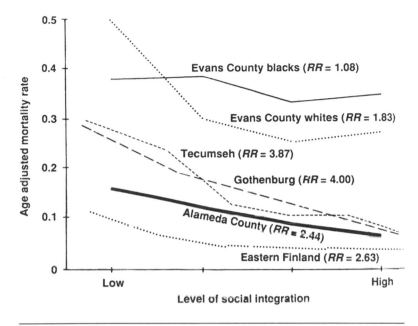

FIG. 35.   Mortality rates and social integration.
(Reprinted with permission from J. S. House, K. Landis, and D. Umberson,
1988, Social Relationships and Health, *Science* 241:540. Copyright © 1988
American Association for the Advancement of Science.)

"blatant acts of violence, verbal harassment, and physical attack combined with subtle and covert slights, accumulated over months, years
and lifetimes, which [have an] impact far more than the sum of individual instances" (Feagin 1991). It has also been suggested that the higher
smoking rates in African Americans may be a stress-reducing behavior,
albeit behavior that is detrimental to physical health (Hummer 1996).

Does It Take a Village?

In a related line of exploration, social scientists have been examining
the reasons for problems that communities and nations have in mutual
cooperation; failures of such cooperation and joint action certainly contribute to many of our recognized social problems in areas such as public education, inner city crime, and environmental global warming. In
such situations, everyone would be better off if there were an increased
degree of cooperation.

Robert Putnam, a sociologist at Harvard, and his colleagues
developed the concept of "social capital" while trying to explain the

successes and failures of some regional governments in Italy since 1970. Those that failed were characterized by inefficiency, lethargy, and corruption, while others were remarkably successful in economic development, community programs, environmental standards, and support for families. Factors such as affluence, political harmony, or ideology, which might have explained the differences, were not found to be significant.

> Surprisingly, the best predictor of effectiveness was what they called "strong traditions of civic engagement," such as voter turnout, newspaper readership, membership in choral societies and literary clubs, and participation in civic organizations and soccer teams (Putnam 1993). They termed this factor *social capital* and described it in an analogous fashion to physical and human capital, as an economic factor that enhances individual productivity.

The term refers to features of social organization such as networks, norms, and trust that facilitate coordination and cooperation for mutual benefit.

While the work of Putnam and his colleagues does not focus on health per se, they note that there have been similar studies that link neighborhood characteristics with teen pregnancy rates in both African Americans and whites, controlling for individual differences; similar factors have been related to coronary artery disease mortality. This is a broader context for the influence of socioeconomic factors, both for health status and for well-being. Indeed, some economists such as Amaryta Sen argue that traditional neoclassical economics with its primary focus on individual economic improvement is limited in explaining individual and community decisions to forgo short-run economic gain for longer benefit to the community or society (Sen 1992). Chapters 7 and 9 will indicate that we are not likely to achieve maximum health outcomes until we are able to devise mechanisms for linking community resources with those of the medical care system, the main task of Purchasing Population Health in phase 3.

How Social Determinants Affect Individual Biology

Although the social determinants of health are not as widely appreciated as medical or biologic ones, the evidence presented in the previous sections is quite compelling. But how do such factors impact on length and quality of life, which are biologic in final effect? Even though there is much in medicine regarding causation that is not certain, basic mechanisms such as cholesterol plaques plugging arteries, cigarette tar causing lung cells to become cancerous, and infectious agents such as viruses destroying certain cell types are generally understood. What similar mechanisms are responsible for the relationship between factors such as social class, income, and social support and resulting mortality and morbidity? How do socioeconomic factors exert a biologic effect?

Stress and Child Development

Most of the evidence on the role of stress comes from animal studies that try to make the link between the socioeconomic environment and individual biology. While it is beyond the scope of this chapter to cover this evidence in great detail (see Evans, Hodge, and Pless 1994), a few examples are helpful. It has long been understood that the body has endocrine mechanisms that respond to stressful situations by increasing output of certain hormones such as adrenaline. This allows us to respond appropriately in times of danger. But there is also evidence that constant stress may eventually result in a lowered capacity of response. In very interesting work, Sapolsky has shown that the mechanism in rats that reduces stress hormone production becomes less effective over time and therefore produces a vicious cycle in which prolonged exposure to stress produces increasing vulnerability to it, accelerating the aging process. In addition, he has found in baboons in Kenya that lower status baboons are less able to turn off the hormone responses to stress and therefore suffer the biologic consequences of higher stress levels (Sapolsky 1990). This finding suggests possible connections to the evidence linking job status with mortality in British civil servants. Marmot has also noted that all job classes have higher blood pressure at work than at home, but the blood pressure of those in higher job classifications drops more at home than that of those in lower grades, suggesting that the former are able to turn off the stress response more effectively (Marmot and Theorell 1988). In other studies in monkeys designed to test coronary artery response to high cholesterol diets, the degree of artery narrowing was four times greater in low status monkeys than in the high status groups (Manuck, Kaplan, and Matthews 1986).

While the precise biological mechanisms for these effects are not fully known, they seem to lie in the interconnected pathways between hormones and the immune system; indeed an entire new area of research has been labeled psycho-neuro-immunology (Reichlin 1993). Enough evidence has already been accumulated to suggest possible biologic pathways for the impact of socioeconomic conditions on health; this should stimulate much more research in this field, as well as blunting the criticism of those who assert that such relationships cannot be important because a feasible mechanism of effect has not been discovered.

It is important in this context to pay special attention to issues in child development, because they influence the entire life span. It is of interest that a companion program to the Population Health Program of the Canadian Institute for Advanced Research is that of Human Development and that efforts are being made to link the efforts of these two groups wherever possible.

It is well understood that early influences can have profound effects on child development at very basic neurological and brain development levels, and more evidence is accumulating as to how these influences play out over the life course. Hertzman points out the important concept of "critical periods" in development (Hertzman 1994), such as are established for primates and other mammals; for example, cats who are not allowed to see out of one eye in the first weeks of life never have vision because the relevant brain regions were not stimulated by light in this "window." In humans, education has been shown to be a protective factor against dementia and decline in mental function in later life (Snowdon et al. 1996).

The Role of Culture

What is culture, and how does it interact with socioeconomic factors and their biological mechanisms? In the previous discussion, the impact of these socioeconomic factors was implicitly assumed to operate at the individual level. But it is also possible that characteristics of the entire society or culture modify the response to various factors. For example, would the same degree of mortality related to job classification be found in societies that are less class conscious than England, where most of the work has been carried out? A comparative study of Britain and Sweden found similar trends in occupational grade and health, but the gradient was much less pronounced (Vagero and Lundberg 1989). Does the historic job security in Japan have anything to do with its lower mortality rates? Are cultures in greater transition from traditional values more prone to direct or indirect socioeconomic effects? Are more diverse and heterogeneous societies the source of increased stress? Does the cultural perspective on a condition, such as mental illness, impact on that culture's definition of health?

The Role of Heredity

Although socioeconomic factors are external to the organism, genetic determinants are deeply embedded within cells and nucleic acid. As illustrated in figure 27, health results from interactions between individuals (genetics and behavior) and their social and physical environments. Baird (1994) has summarized three types of circumstances linking genetics and disease:

- The individual has genes that cannot adapt to ordinary environments (cystic fibrosis, hemophilia).
- A hostile environment overwhelms the genetic adaptive capacity (viruses, toxins).
- A combination of environmental insult and genetic predisposition results in disease (diabetes, heart disease).

She illustrates the complexity of these interactions with the example of individuals with early heart attacks due to high cholesterol. At one extreme there are individuals who have a genetically determined metabolism that causes symptoms even when cholesterol levels in diets are normal. The other extreme is those whose metabolism of cholesterol is intact but whose very heavy cholesterol intake (environment) overwhelms normal metabolic mechanisms. If dietary cholesterol is low in the culture or subpopulation, the percentage of cases from genetic metabolic factors will necessarily be greater.

Because of such interactions, in addition to the way mortality is classified (anatomic site, for example), it is not possible to quantify precisely the contribution of genetic factors to death and disease. However, the following is a list of some of the best understood genetic contributions:

- Many failed pregnancies are the result of genetic abnormalities and chromosome defects.
- Five percent of individuals have a disease of genetic origin significant enough to require treatment before age 25.
- Infant mortality is now one-third from genetic causes.

· Over age 25, more than 60 percent of diseases of late onset may
have genetics as one contributing factor.

Baird points out that classically Mendelian genetic disorders,
which reduce the life span and cause psychological handicaps, are primarily found in early life, with 90 percent appearing by the end of
puberty. In later life, genetic variability of populations decreases as
those with the least adaptive genes die, leaving most of the remaining
elderly with nongenetic disease.

The field of genetic epidemiology is concerned with the reasons
diseases cluster in families and ethnic groups, and it tries to determine
whether the clustering is caused by common environmental exposure,
biologically inherited susceptibility, and/or culturally inherited risk
factors (King et al. 1984; Morton 1993). Using creative methods such as
twin studies, adoption studies, and migration studies, some of these
genetic and environmental factors can be separated. Hereditary factors
have been identified for schizophrenia, alcoholism, and high blood
pressure; examples of genetic factors are found in sickle cell anemia,
Down's syndrome, and susceptibility to malaria.

There is significant controversy about whether or to what degree
intervention in the genetic makeup of individuals and populations
would be an effective or acceptable strategy for increasing population
health. The excitement of the Human Genome Project and the initial
experiments in laboratory animals raise the possibility that altering the
frequency of some genes in individuals or populations would contribute to future population health improvement. But there are several
lines of caution in placing major emphasis on this approach. The first is
that the genetic reservoir of variation is one way that the species evolves
and deals with future environmental change. Tampering with this in an
attempt to create genetic endowments that are "ideal" is risky, if not
fraught with ethical considerations. In addition, most genetic disorders
are complex multigene interactions, which we are far from being able to
manipulate in humans. Finally, the impact on mortality and morbidity
is very often the result of interactions between host susceptibility and
environmental influences, including lifestyle. It is likely that for many
genetic diseases, the environmental factors may be quicker and less
costly to change. Having said that, we should proceed with basic research into the potential for genetic change, while the therapeutic potential of genetic change should be judged by the same marginal benefit
investment framework that will be developed for all determinants of
health in chapter 6.

TABLE 12. Actual Causes of Death in the United States in 1990

	Deaths	
Cause	Estimated Number	Percentage of Total Deaths
Tobacco	400,000	19
Diet/activity patterns	300,000	14
Alcohol	100,000	5
Microbial agents	90,000	4
Toxic agents	60,000	3
Firearms	35,000	2
Sexual behavior	30,000	1
Motor vehicles	25,000	1
Illicit use of drugs	20,000	<1
Total	1,060,000	50

Source: Reprinted with permission from McGinnis and Foege 1993, Courtesy of *JAMA* 270:2207–12.

Environment: The World around Us

Environmental health is an entire field and discipline in its own right, with academic units, journals, advocacy groups, and regulatory legislation. It is one of the determinants of health but also makes contributions to general well-being and quality of life, in terms of aesthetics and recreation. Efforts directed toward environmental protection and restoration have been a major social movement of the late twentieth century, drawing the attention of people concerned about the future of the world in which they live. The Trout Unlimited motto, "We All Live Downstream," and the national park challenge, "Leave No Trace," capture the concerns of an increasing number of Americans.

The field of environmental health is a broad one, dealing both with the impact of the environment on people and that of people on the environment (Moeller 1992; Koren 1995). Components include air, water, and food quality, waste disposal, rodents and insects, injury control, radiation, workplace safety, and issues concerning energy sources and use. Both short- and long-term considerations such as global warming and acid rain are encompassed.

With regard to health outcomes, the Centers for Disease Control and Prevention have estimated (McGinnis and Foege 1993) a range of 57,000 to 108,000 deaths in 1990 (3 to 6 percent of all deaths) that could be attributed to what they term *toxic agents* (not including tobacco, alcohol, and dietary components), as shown in table 12.

These pose threats as occupational hazards, environmental pollutants, contaminants of food and water supplies, and components of commercial products. These agents are known to have an impact on all organ systems, including the heart, lungs, liver, kidneys, bladder, and nervous system. Cancer deaths from environmental or occupational exposure are estimated at 30,000 annually, including 9,000 from asbestos.

The nonfatal effect (morbidity) of such toxic exposure is more difficult to measure but is perhaps more important than mortality. For example, lead poisoning is rarely fatal, but the neurologic and mental damage to the more than 230,000 children having high blood lead levels is certainly significant. Asthma kills about 5,000 people per year but also contributes significantly to absence from school and work (O'Neill 1996); for asthma a major risk factor or trigger is air pollution as well as cockroaches in the living environment (Platts-Mills and Carter 1997). Reproductive outcomes are impacted by eating contaminated fish (Dar et al. 1992). We are all aware of disease and morbidity caused by food impurity, by water contamination, and by workplace injury. Ostro (1983) showed that a 10 percent increase in the total suspended particles in urban air samples resulted in a 4.5 percent increase in the number of workdays lost, and Mullahy and Portney (1990) were able to show that increased cigarette consumption was about 2.5 times more important in causing restricted activity than increases in ozone concentration. There is evidence that environmental quality varies by race and income, with lower socioeconomic groups having higher exposure to toxic wastes and air pollution (Brown 1995).

With current efforts for environmental cleanup gaining public attention (for example, cleanup procedures that have led to the return of Great Lakes fish stocks), perhaps it is possible to reduce vigilance in this area. However, more subtle environmental "sentinels" in wildlife, particularly regarding hormonal changes, are cause for concern. Broader environmental issues such as ozone depletion and global warming may have health and social consequences that are not yet fully appreciated.

The field of environmental health has also provided us with some of the best analytic methods regarding exposure and risk and long-run cost benefit analysis; an example is shown in chapter 6, table 15. In addition, working toward environmental outcomes is cited in chapter 7 as one promising model for public-private cross-sectoral collaboration for outcome improvement.

Is Health an Individual Responsibility?

Are individuals responsible for the health consequences of their own behavior? Up to this point the determinants of health such as medical care and socioeconomic factors have been presented as impacting on the population as a whole. Are individuals passive in the face of these determinants, or do they have independent roles to play? In the Evans and Stoddart model of producing health outcomes (fig. 27), the role of individual behavior is identified as being important in its own right.

In a 1977 classic collection of essays titled *Doing Better and Feeling Worse: Health in the United States,* John Knowles, M.D., president of the Rockefeller Foundation, said, "over 99 percent of us are born healthy, and made sick as a result of personal misbehavior and environmental conditions. The solution to the problems of ill health in modern American society involves individual responsibility in the first instance, and social responsibility . . . in the second" (Knowles 1977). Early studies from this period identified the importance of the following "basic health habits" as contributing to health and life expectancy: three meals a day, moderate exercise two to three times per week, adequate sleep, no smoking, reasonable weight, and alcohol in moderation.

In the current cause of death statistics from the Centers for Disease Control and Prevention (table 12), the three leading causes of death (tobacco, diet/activity, and alcohol use) are rooted in behavioral choices, as are others on the list such as use of firearms, sexual activity, motor vehicle accidents, and illicit drug use. *Healthy People 2000,* the 1990 statement of health goals for the nation, included eight behaviors that required improvement for health promotion: physical activity and fitness; awareness of nutrition and the hazards of tobacco, alcohol, and other drugs; family planning; dentificated treatment of mental health and emotional disorders; avoidance of violent and abusive behavior; and establishment of community-based education programs. A 1995 report on mid-decade progress on these goals noted substantial reduction in adult tobacco use and alcohol-related automobile deaths and a modest improvement in diet but no reductions in sedentary lifestyle or weight (McGinnis and Lee 1995).

What limits improvement in individual behavior change? Knowles listed several reasons in 1977: the denial of death coupled with demand for instant gratification; the belief that science and technology will conquer nature; chronic depression causing disinterest or inactivity; and the focus of medicine and physicians on cure rather than prevention. Such factors are supported by current anecdotal information that the availability of new AIDS protease inhibitor drugs has resulted in an increase of unsafe sex practices.

Some health behaviorists and public health educators are beginning to think much more broadly about such challenges, applying strategies of "social marketing" to sophisticated public health communication (Maibach and Holtgrave 1995). This entails strategies such as targeting messages to homogeneous audiences, presenting information about risks from behavioral choices, developing mass media advocacy, building information strategies into entertainment programming, and encouraging the use of computer interactive patient education programs for sensitive topics like sexual behavior (Gustafson et al. 1987; Chewning 1993). Some evidence of progress in behavior change has been noted recently. Providing consumers with information and guidelines about self-care and increasing their confidence about making medical decisions can be effective; in addition, health promotion in the workplace has been shown to reduce absenteeism and medical care expenditures.

In the area of prevention and health promotion, it is not the lack of scientific knowledge that limits us, but our ability to apply existing knowledge. This is difficult, because in many cases we are dealing with fundamental issues of values, beliefs, culture, and individual rights. Wikler (1992) provides a quote from Craig Claiborne, food editor of the *New York Times,* that highlights the challenge:

> I love hamburgers and chile con carne and hot dogs. And foie gras and those small birds known as ortolans. I love banquettes of quail eggs with hollandaise sauce and clambakes with lobsters dipped in so much butter it dribbles down the chin. I like cheesecake and crepes filled with cream sauces and strawberries with cream fraiche . . .
>
> And if I am abbreviating my stay on this earth for an hour or so, I say only that I have no desire to be a Methuselah, a hundred or more years old and still alive, grace be to something that plugs into an electric outlet.

From an ethical perspective, Wikler reminds us that smoking, sloth, or other dangerous but enjoyable pastimes are still the decision of each individual, although as a society we have decided that certain behaviors such as driving at any speed or without seat belts or having medicine in non-childproof containers are not optional.

Scientific advances in behavioral change strategies will be as important in the twenty-first century as those in biomedicine were in the twentieth. Delbanco says it for preventive medical care: "There are lots of studies analyzing the beneficial effects of universal sigmoidoscopy . . . but try to find one that tells you the best way to get a man or woman to bare his or her bottom on a periodic basis to a large tube" (Delbanco 1996).

But health improvement is not an individual responsibility alone. Certain aspects, noted by Knowles, are a social responsibility, and the individual cannot solely be blamed for the poor health of the population. There are, for example, strong economic interests such as the tobacco industry that counter the efforts of health promotion.

> **In addition, there are segments of society, many of low education and income, whose lives are desperate and for whom such imperatives such as good nutrition are remote or economically impossible. For these reasons there is societal as well as individual responsibility for health behavior change, and a combined strategy is required if optimal progress in improving population health outcomes is to be achieved.**

The Role of Public Health

Many in health care will be surprised that the role of public health has not been mentioned so far in this book. I admit to some definitional confusion at this point, but I am not alone in this quandary. The Institute of Medicine (IOM) defined the mission of public health as "fulfilling society's interest in assuring conditions in which people can be healthy" (Institite of Medicine 1988); Breslow states that it does this by "encouraging action of others in public and private sectors, by regulation requiring action, and by providing direct services" (Breslow 1990). Afifi and Breslow define the core disciplines of public health as epidemiology, biostatistics, personal health services, health behavior, and environmental health and define public health practice as "those actions that are directed to the assessment of health and disease in the population, the formulation of policies for dealing with such problems, and the assurance of environmental, behavioral, and medical services designed to accelerate favorable health trends and reduce the unfavorable" (Afifi and Breslow 1994).

Most of the interventions and services classically thought of in public health have been accounted for in the Evans and Stoddart framework for this chapter: medical care, the physical environment, the social environment, genetics, and the role of individual behavior. During the health reform debate in 1993 and 1994, the expectation of universal coverage for personal health services led to active discussion of "reinventing public health" in a post–universal coverage world (Lee and Toomey 1994), since this critical safety net personal health provider role to the uninsured and geographically isolated would have been assumed by the proposed alliances and plans. Since universal coverage remains an unfilled priority, the role of public health as a critical provider of last resort remains.

But for the majority of insured Americans, almost all of their personal care is provided outside of the traditional state and local public health systems, causing definitional confusion since the role that medical care plays in health status is then not primarily in the "public" sector. Sommer has asked, "why have we meekly accepted the restrictive, traditional public health agency dominated mold the IOM prepared for us?" He proposes a "modest response: expunge the words public health . . . which carry too much baggage . . . and speak instead of a complex, diverse, integrated, and dynamic enterprise, composed of many disciplines, whose goal is protecting and improving the health of the public." He continues that "a capitated care system, which is rapidly evolving in this country, should care for the entire population . . . the job of public health should be to ensure that everyone's health in that capitated system is maximized" (Sommer 1995).

Certainly public health departments have critical core population based roles in environmental services and protection. Given their expertise in community prevention activities, they also have essential roles for public education, behavior change, and outreach services to high-risk populations. If a fundamental role is the "assurance of healthy conditions," then an expanding core function of public health agencies has to be in the data collection or monitoring function for measuring population health improvement (see chapter 4). It is also possible that public health agencies at the state or local level could provide the coordinating mechanisms across the multiple determinants of health, assuming the leadership role of the Health Outcomes Trust presented in chapter 9.

There has a been a recent vigorous discussion of the need for closer working relationships between medicine and public health (Rundall 1994; Reiser 1996). The Centers for Disease Control and Prevention established a Managed Care Working Group to "foster the incorporation of prevention practices into managed care" (CDCP 1995). The Robert Wood Johnson Foundation and the Kellogg Foundation have established their "Turning Point" program to foster such collaboration, and the New York Academy of Medicine has held a symposium and will be publishing a monograph in the fall of 1997 containing more than 500 specific examples of collaboration across medicine and public health.

But if public health is to reinvent its role, the weakened system needs to be strengthened. "Distinct policies are needed to strengthen the infrastructure for delivering population-based services at the state and local levels and to encourage the public and personal health care systems to work constructively together. The public health system is uniquely qualified to provide population-based community health services. However without expanding health insurance coverage, the public health system will not be able to move away from providing medical care to the indigent and uninsured and the infrastructure will continue to deteriorate" (Lee and Paxman 1997).

The Purchasing Population Health framework therefore could be thought of as closely related to the "health of the public," but considering public health agencies as having an independent role for some functions and working in collaboration for others.

Short Term vs. Long Term

The child development considerations discussed earlier lead to the generic consideration of latency, highlighted by Hertzman and colleagues (Hertzman, Frank, and Evans 1994). This concept recognizes that different factors influencing population health status have their impact over different time periods; that is, an epidemic, a new immunization, or a new form of hip replacement might have immediate impact, while education is presumably gained primarily in childhood, with impact over a lifetime. He cites the report of Barker and Osmond (1987) describing three English towns with different mortality rates but similar socioeconomic profiles, which would be unexpected according to what we have learned about the socioeconomic gradient. Since the towns were in the same region with similar health resources, it is unlikely that different environments or medical services were the explanation for the variation in mortality rates. Table 13 shows data for these three towns.

There was a parallel relationship in 1911 between infant mortality rates and crowded housing, an indicator of socioeconomic status.

TABLE 13. Mortality in Three English Towns

	1911–13		1968–71	1911	1911	1971
	Infant Mortality	Standardized Mortality	Infant Mortality	% Greater than 2/Room	% Greater than 1/Room	% Lower Occupation Class
Burnley	177	121	22	9.5	14	75
Colne	130	109	19	6.6	10	74
Nelson	87	100	20	3.7	14	75
England/Wales	111		18	9.1	12	65

Source: Data from Barker and Osmond 1987.

Other anecdotal information confirms this gradient in 1911. The all-cause mortality in 1968–71 follows the same pattern, but the infant mortality rates in this latter period do not show these differences. By 1971, the socioeconomic status of the three towns had become similar, as measured by occupations and the percentage of persons living with more than one person per room. This gives credence to the suggestion that it was the previous 1911, not the current 1971, relative socioeconomic status that was associated with current overall mortality differences in the three towns.

It is almost definitional that changes in life expectancy will occur in the long run, whether they are the result of medical or non-medical factors. The result is that future cohorts will have greater (or less) future life expectancy than previous cohorts of similar age. Even if changes in life expectancy were the result of prevention in the medical care system such as lowering cholesterol levels, the resulting improvement would be detected only in future years. Furthermore, morbidity is likely to be more amenable to intervention in the short run (e.g., hip replacement or treatment of depression) than mortality. In some cases, interventions might have impact on both life expectancy and morbidity (e.g., prenatal care and social support reducing low-birth-weight babies or a drug with short-term benefit and long-term side effects) and therefore would need to be measured in both the short run and the long run. A mechanism for measuring both short- and long-term impact needs to be a part of the Purchasing Population Health financial incentive structure and is discussed in chapter 9.

In economic terms, such future investment considerations are called discounting or time preference. Drummond and colleagues indicate that "even in a world with zero inflation or no interest, it would be an advantage to receive a benefit earlier or a cost later," since resources spent now are not available for other investment (Drummond, Stoddart, and Torrance 1987). Sheldon points out that the choice of discount rate is fraught with difficulty and imprecision and notes that higher discount rates will "inevitably favor the immediate health gains obtained from curative health services" at the expense of longer term and preventive programs (Sheldon 1992). Additional work on time preference rates such as those of Cairns (1992) and Dolan and Gudex (1995) is needed to determine how such factors should be incorporated into a Purchasing Population Health perspective. This has been considered recently by the United States Public Health Service Panel on Cost Effectiveness in Health and Medicine, which recommended that a "base rate of 3% and an alternative rate of 5% be retained for ten years" (Gold et al. 1996).

Summary

This chapter has shown that a host of medical and nonmedical factors is involved in producing health outcomes. All of these factors are critical; we cannot improve population health without each making its unique contribution. The relationships we have discussed so far deal with each one independently, but this is an oversimplified analysis.

> **If an optimal allocation of societal resources for improving health outcomes is desired, we not only have to understand the interactions, but the relative costs associated with each, so that health output can be maximized for the resources available.**

If resources were not limited, we would not have to deal with the cost-effectiveness question and could just continue to blindly increase the investments in all determinants, until no more health output seemed possible. But resources are limited and will be for the forseeable future, perhaps to an increasing degree. The next chapter will deal with these issues and will develop a framework for an optimal investment strategy across determinants in a world of limited resources.

6 · Can Rationing Be Rational?
Balancing the Determinants of Health

The clinician is obliged to do everything for his or her patient
that is cost effective. If a clinician exceeds his or her brief and
delivers care that is merely effective, scarce resources will be
wasted and patients. . . . will be deprived of cost-effective
care from which they could benefit.
 —Alan Maynard, 1995

It is not helpful simply to define the problem away through
judicious code words, pretending thereafter that the rationing of
health care can be avoided forever in the United States. The
nation has not been able to avoid rationing in the past, and will
not be able to avoid it in the future. The nation has merely lacked
the courage to admit rationing forthrightly and to debate the
merits of alternative forms of rationing in good faith.
 —Uwe Reinhardt, 1996

Until now, the multiple factors that impact on health status have been
considered independently and in isolation from each other. This is a
useful way to begin to understand them, but in the real world they act
together and interact simultaneously. We need to consider the issue of
the relative cost of and return from investing in alternate determinants.
If we wish to purchase population health more effectively by altering
the investment strategy across determinants, it is necessary to understand both how these interactions take place and the relative cost-
effectiveness of each factor. In economics this is referred to as the
"production function," and the analytic tools for understanding these
relationships come primarily from economic concepts and methods
such as cost-effectiveness analysis, marginal return, substitution, and
rationing. Each of these will be developed and illustrated in this chapter, as we look at how investments in the different determinants might
be balanced.

Are We Rationing Now?

Rationing is a term with multiple definitions, and it is often used with
imprecision. Although it can be and has been used polemically as a
scare tactic to quickly label and kill some idea or program, its dictionary

definition is "to distribute and divide (as commodities in short supply) in an equitable manner or so as to achieve a particular object (as maximum production of a particular item)" (*Webster's* 1976). A common type of rationing occurs in times of war or famine when basic necessities are allocated on some criterion of need or merit rather than the ability to pay. In health care, common usage of the term implies either implicitly or explicitly that some individuals do not receive services that are either needed or desired.

In the United States we have not yet decided if health care is a public or a private good, and therefore we ration on the ability to pay. As one of our leading medical ethicists, Norman Daniels, has stated,

> **our rationing system excludes whole categories of poor and near poor from access to insurance, denying coverage to people, rather than (denying) low-priority services. (Daniels 1991)**

This results in the 16 percent of U.S. citizens without basic health insurance, a number that grows every year. But denial of service can occur within the insured population as well: babies on Medicaid have been shown to receive fewer services than those with private insurance, and in one study 63 percent of Medicaid patients were denied care simply because they were on Medicaid. Many individuals with private insurance have to pay fully or partially for such items as medications or glasses, and so rationing can also be seen as a continuum.

While some U.S. citizens still believe that health care is a commodity like bread and housing to be distributed according to ability to pay, many feel otherwise. Health economist Uwe Reinhardt poses the following question:

> Assume that a scarce health care resource (a transplantable organ, a highly skilled surgeon, or a dialysis machine) could be allocated to only one of two patients: one the child of a low-income gas station attendant and the other the child of a wealthy executive. Should that scarce resource be allocated to the child whose family is able to bid the highest money price for it? (Reinhardt 1996)

Reinhardt asserts that neither most U.S. citizens nor most economists would agree with this conclusion.

But if not by ability to pay, then how should allocation take place? We live in a world of limited resources, and previous chapters have provided evidence that slower rates of growth or even reductions in health expenditures are possible. Is there a rational basis for allocating scarce health care resources, rather than arbitrarily using the ability to pay? The Purchasing Population Health argument says yes from a utilitarian perspective, in which increasing health adjusted life expectancy to the maximum amount per dollar invested would become the private and public purchasing standard in the future. Chapter 8 will discuss the important issues of populations with different "needs" for health resources; for now we will consider the general issue of cost-effectiveness across the multiple determinants of health.

Determining Cost-Effectiveness in Health

In general, cost-effectiveness is an economic evaluation that identifies costs and effectiveness of treatments, technologies, or programs. This assumes that resource constraints are at work, either through competitive market forces or regulatory limits on expenditures. For the assessment of each intervention, measures of both cost and health impact are required, as well as equivalent comparisons of two or more alternatives. The final purpose of such an economic evaluation is to make choices possible between alternative courses of action (Drummond, Stoddart, and Torrance 1987; Weinstein et al. 1996; Gold et al. 1996).

Much cost-effectiveness analysis in health care has proceeded by using concepts like QALYs or similar measures introduced in chapter 4 and illustrated in figure 22. A growing body of research on the cost-effectiveness of different medical interventions allows the construction of cost-effectiveness "league tables" such as illustrated in table 14.

This list of only seven medical interventions shows that there is a considerable range of cost per life year saved, from $3,777 for smoking counseling to $88,057 for coronary artery bypass grafts in patients with moderate angina (Phelps 1997). This list also demonstrates that similar interventions have different cost-effectiveness, depending on patient characteristics. Coronary artery bypass grafts are more cost effective if the disease is more severe, as is neonatal intensive care for infants of higher birth weight. Some interventions like immunization and PKU screening are even more cost effective than those shown here, while many high technology procedures are even less effective. These studies are complex and need to be done with great care in terms of the measures of cost and benefit, as well as with regard to whether the intervention is compared to doing nothing or to an alternate intervention. While

TABLE 14.   Estimated Cost-Effectiveness Ratios of Commonly Used Medical Interventions

Intervention	Cost/Life Year (1993 $)
MD advice about smoking	3,777
Coronary artery bypass grafts, left main	8,768
Neonatal intensive care (1,000–1,500 g)	10,927
Annual breast exam (55–65)	15,243
Annual breast exam (55–65) with mammography	41,008
Neonatal intensive care (500–999 g)	77,161
Coronary artery bypass grafts, moderate angina	88,057

Source: Reprinted with permission from Phelps 1997.

table 14 is only for life years gained, many analyses have been done with QALYs in which the quality of the life years gained is measured as well (Drummond, Stoddart, and Torrance 1987).

Comparing the Cost-Effectiveness of Different Investments

The second important economic concept of relevance is that of diminishing marginal return, which was introduced in chapter 3. Data on cross-national relationships between life expectancy and per capita income (fig. 15) showed that at higher levels of per capita income, relatively less gain in life expectancy is achieved for each additional unit of income.

Such a relationship is similarly illustrated in figure 36 for health expenditures in the United States over time. Not only is there a decline in mortality when the percentage of GDP increases, but the declines slow at higher levels of percentage of GDP in the later years. Such changes are called "marginal" when expressed as the amount of change in comparison to additional resources. The figure also demonstrates the law of diminishing marginal returns, which states that as one factor is increased, proportional increase in total output starts to fall at some point. This data shows that for each succeeding 2 percent increase in percentage of GDP spent on health, less reduction in mortality resulted (a reduction of 131 years going from 4 to 6 percent of GDP but only 20 years from 12 percent to 14 percent). Of course, this does not mean that health expenditure is the only reason for the mortality improvement, and it does not speak to declines in morbid-

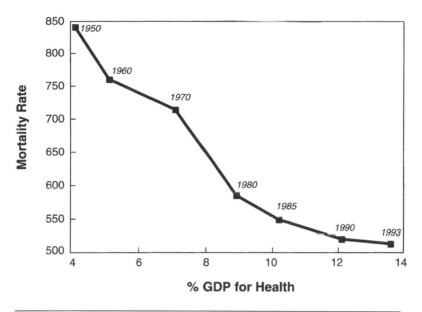

FIG. 36. Mortality and U.S. health expenditure.
(Data from USDHHS 1996.)

ity, which probably would show similar relationships but are not demonstrated here.

The Health Production Function

We will now consider this concept in the context of multiple factors for improving health outcomes. Figure 37 illustrates a health outcome "production function" and demonstrates cost-effectiveness and rationing issues. The vertical axis is the outcome of population health, measured in HALEs. The horizontal axis is units of health producing investments. The maximum health that can be reached is at point A, which takes the consumption of four units of resources. There is no rationale for patients, providers, or payers to make investments to the right of point A to point B; this is the area where the ineffective or inappropriate expenditures discussed in chapter 3 are located. Of course sometimes excessive levels of treatment themselves cause poor health ("iatrogenic" effects), which explains why the line could bend downward after this point to point C.

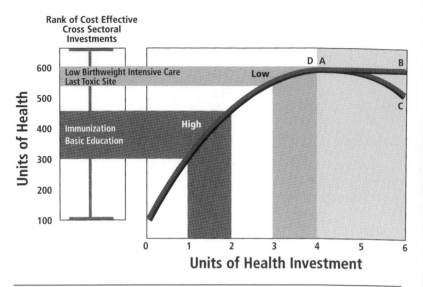

FIG. 37.   Health investment and health outcome.

Figure 37 can help us think through rationing and how it applies to our concerns about equity in the distribution of health. Rationing would certainly not apply to limiting expenditures to the right of
point A, since these are not useful in producing additional health and
should be considered "luxury" expenditures, which individuals with
private resources could purchase if they wish. Many persons in the
United States and other countries have avoided the rationing discussion
altogether, assuming that there were enough ineffective expenditures to
the right of point A that significant reductions in costs could be made
without dealing with expenditures of limited effectiveness.

Until recently, I allowed myself this point of view, but the need
for resources elsewhere in the health care system (such as covering the
uninsured for basic care) or elsewhere in society has made me question
whether we can afford highly expensive services that have a very small
degree of benefit. To quote the classic treatise on cost-effectiveness by
Weinstein and Stason:

> Alternative programs or services are then ranked, from the
> lowest value of this cost effectiveness ratio to the highest, and
> are selected until available resources are exhausted. The point
> on the priority list at which available resources are exhausted,
> or for which society is no longer willing to pay the price for the

benefits achieved, becomes society's cutoff level of permissible cost-per-unit effectiveness. (Weinstein and Stason 1977)

A recent editorial in the *British Medical Journal* says it this way:

No doubt substantial sums can eventually be saved by stopping ineffective interventions, but there are increasing examples of treatments which have proved effective but are hugely expensive when given to certain sorts of patients [where capacity to benefit is severely limited]. . . . These last drops of effectiveness are available at unaffordable costs, which means that decisions must be made to deny some people effective treatments. (Smith 1996).

This is a rational approach to rationing, and it is defined as explicitly limiting expenditures that fall to the left of point A. The first items to be eliminated would be those at point D that contribute the least marginal return to health outcomes. Actually, the vertical axis on figure 37 can be considered a QALY league table (such as table 14) with neonatal intensive care for low-birth-weight babies hypothetically at the top (least cost effective in terms of health improvement per dollar) and immunization at the bottom (most cost effective). Since this axis includes all health producing investments, the health gain from investments in sectors like education and environment has been represented in terms of high return from basic education and low return from cleaning up the last and most difficult toxic waste site.

The black area contains those interventions of higher marginal cost-effectiveness than those in the gray zone. In this rationing model, most attention needs to be paid to the "flat of the curve" investments just to the left of point A, where almost no benefit is gained from additional resources. Of course, over time new items will be added to the vertical axis, and existing ones will change in their relative cost-effectiveness as biologic and social science and implementation strategies evolve, and so it should not be thought of as a static but rather as a constantly evolving strategy.

Balancing Competing Investments

It is easier to determine production function curves as described previously for manufacturing than for population health, where the processes are more complex and the available data is quite limited. In order to establish how different factors interact to produce health, there must be a large number of populations with different health outcomes and differing amounts of the various determinants of health, so that across all of these variations the significant contribution of each factor can be established. Cross-national studies can attempt this, but often different measures of inputs such as education and social services confound the analysis. Variations across geographic areas can be used, but even 50 different states might not introduce enough variation to show meaningful differences. With even smaller populations, data is limited for factors such as medical care expenditures or levels of other determinants such as education, social services, and the environment.

There have been several attempts to overcome these difficulties. Using multivariate regression statistical techniques, it is possible to approximate the independent effects of multiple variables interacting together. Such models are complex from a statistical perspective, as well as from the theory that drives the analysis (Zweifel and Breyer 1997). Depending on the specific groups that are studied and the sources of data, it has been found that medical care, income, education, and smoking all have significant independent relationships to health status. While specific findings vary, several studies indicate that factors such as educational level are as important as medical care expenditures in reducing mortality (Grossman 1972; Auster 1969; Hadley 1982; Wolfe 1986). Although this confirms some of the findings from examining the factors separately as we did earlier, there are not yet adequate studies to provide precise guidelines about the relative effectiveness of investments across determinants. It is also not clear that the balance of factors explaining past outcomes will be the same as those for future improvement.

Almost no work has been done on assessing the effect of the nonmedical determinants of health or in comparing them to those in medical care. One notable exception is the study by Michael Drummond and colleagues in York, England, and Hamilton and Toronto, Canada. These researchers identified the cost of improvement in quality of life for the caregivers of demented elderly persons who had the aid of a specially designed Caregiver Support Program. The cost of a QALY gained for caregivers was priced at about $20,000 (Drummond et al. 1991). A similar approach has been used in comparing the cost-effectiveness of 500 lifesaving interventions, ranging from a number of medical procedures to injury reduction strategies to toxin control, as shown in table 15.

For the categories of interventions studied here, on average medical procedures cost $19,000 per life year saved; fatal injury reduction averaged $48,000; toxic waste control had much higher costs than

TABLE 15. Cost/Life Year Saved Estimates as a Function of Sector of Society and Type of Intervention

| Sector of Society | Type of Intervention | | | |
	Medicine	Fatal Injury Reduction	Toxin Control	All
Health care	$19,000 (n = 310)	N/A	N/A	$19,000 (n = 310)
Residential	N/A	$36,000 (n = 30)	N/A	$36,000 (n = 30)
Transportation	N/A	$56,000 (n = 87)	N/A	$56,000 (n = 87)
Occupational	N/A	$68,000 (n = 16)	$1,388,000 (n = 20)	$346,000 (n = 36)
Environmental	N/A	N/A	$4,207,000 (n = 124)	$4,207,000 (n = 124)
All	$19,000 (n = 133)	$48,000 (n = 133)	$2,782,000 (n = 144)	$42,000 (n = 587)

Source: Reprinted with permission from Tengs et al. 1995, from *Risk Analysis* 15 (3): 369–90.
Note: All medians are rounded to the nearest thousand dollars.

either of the first two interventions (Tengs et al. 1995). None of the socioeconomic factors discussed earlier in this chapter was examined in this study. Such work is in its infancy, and much more needs to be learned in order to guide individual, corporate, and public investment.

A Rational Approach to Rationing

The Oregon Plan

Although these concepts are complicated and can be difficult to implement, there is one U.S. example of public decision making based on cost-effectiveness analysis. The State of Oregon recently used such an approach in determining how it would limit services provided in its Medicaid program, with the resources saved being used to provide basic coverage for more of their uninsured.

The Oregon Health Services Act of 1989 provided for expanding the Medicaid program to all legal residents with incomes below the federal poverty level but required a prioritized list of covered services; those services falling below the legislatively determined cutoff line would not be provided at all in order to provide the higher priority

TABLE 16. List of "Essential" Condition-Treatment (CT) Pairs Moved Below Line 587 and CT Pairs "Valuable to Certain Individuals" Moved Above Line 587 in the Oregon Plan

Rank	Category	Condition	Treatment
"Essential" CT pairs that are not covered			
606	3	Hepatorenal syndrome	Medical therapy
607	5	Other deficiencies of circulating enzymes (alpha 1-antitrypsin deficiency)	Lung transplant
608	5	Lethal midline granuloma	Medical therapy
609	5	Amyotrophic lateral scleorsis (ALS)	Medical therapy
610	5	Cancer of liver and intrahepatic bile ducts	Liver transplant
687	2	Intraventricular and subarachnoid hemorrhage of fetus or neonate	Medical therapy
690	5	Alcoholic cirrhosis of liver	Liver transplant
691	5	Non-Hodgkin's lymphomas	Bone marrow transplant (5–6 loci match)
CT pairs "valuable to certain individuals" that are covered			
352	14	Pilonidal cyst with abscess	Medical and surgical treatment
358	14	Acute conjunctivitis	Medical therapy
396	14	Infective otitis externa	Medical therapy
424	17	Ophthalmic injury: Lacrimal system laceration	Closure
434	14	Body infestations (e.g., lice, scabies)	Medical therapy

Source: Reprinted with permission from Office of Technology Assessment 1992.

services to the expanded population. A Health Services Commission of providers and consumers was appointed, with the charge of determining "basic health care" services that would become the "floor beneath which no individual should fall." In addition to examining scientific data on effectiveness and cost (a sort of QALY league table as described earlier), individual and community views were elicited through a series of phone interviews and community forums. The commission reviewed all the data and made adjustments by moving services above or below the Condition-Treatment Pair #589 cutoff line. Table 16 shows some of the 30 services from the original "scientific" list that were moved from the covered category to the uncovered category as a result of this process (Office of Technology Assessment 1992).

Using figure 37 as a point of reference, we can say that the commission decided not to pay for a set of services to the left of point A that was determined to be of too little benefit for the cost; resources saved allowed access to medical treatments to a larger number of persons, though all were limited to those services with a higher marginal return per dollar invested.

Whereas the Oregon Plan has been criticized on many fronts, it is also acknowledged as one of the first attempts to use the concepts and tools of cost-effectiveness and marginal return in public policy decisions (Eddy 1991a,b; Hadorn 1991; Daniels 1991). For expanded use such as Purchasing Population Health, more sophisticated criteria and processes for making such social judgments will have to be developed and specified.

A "Military Base Closing" Analogy

Some legislators have openly discussed the difficulty of denying benefits with any degree of effectiveness (such as in the Oregon Plan) and/or those that have no benefits but are extremely popular with voters. This has led to a series of insurance mandates at the state level, some of which may be reasonable (such as a minimum 48 hour hospitalization for maternity care) but some of which (such as mandates for experimental procedures with as yet limited or no benefits) constrain insurers and health plans in their efforts to limit costs. As Purchasing Population Health matures, perhaps a blue ribbon public-private commission could be given the responsibility for deciding which investments have zero or limited value (benefit for resources expended), so that private or public payers would not be advised or required to purchase them. Such an approach could initially be adopted for Medicare and Medicaid, which would operate like a "military model base closing," so that legislators could not add or remove individual items but rather simply would approve or reject the entire list. Decisions made for Medicare in such a public process might later be adopted as guidelines for private purchasers. To be effective and fair, such a process should incorporate legal safeguards for individuals and organizations following these guidelines, to protect them from the threat of malpractice and to reduce the costs of defensive medicine that our existing legal framework encourages.

We Can Get More for Less

David Eddy has done a great deal to advance the cost-effectiveness and rational rationing imperative in a series of articles that appeared in the

Journal of the American Medical Association from 1990 to 1994. In one titled "Rationing Resources while Improving Quality: How to Get More for Less" (Eddy 1994), he develops the following list:

The Things We Will Need to Do:
- Accept once and for all that resources are limited.
- Help patients understand the consequences of limits and the need to be fair.
- Change from qualitative thinking (any potential benefit) to quantitative thinking (the most benefit per dollar); the physician corollary is the following: "When in doubt, don't."
- Focus on populations rather than individuals. Resources wasted on ineffective treatments for one individual do not come from insurers or administrators but rather from other patients.
- Measures of quality need to support the strategy for increasing outcomes while decreasing costs.

Summary

This chapter has described ways of considering which investments produce better health outcomes and how to develop and implement a rationing model in an era of limited resources. The possibility of greater return for health as well as for social cohesion and economic productivity resulting from a better balance of investments in times of constrained resources is more than speculative. Further chapters will address the managerial opportunities and challenges in bringing about such cost-effectiveness. But knowledge must precede action, even if it does not ensure it. In the area of analyzing the balance of determinants of health status, it is urgent that the relative returns to health from different investments be accurately determined. Once this is done, we will have to find ways to integrate these investments across the multiple determinants of health. The next chapter will explore the challenges in managing such sectoral boundaries for optimal effectiveness.

7 · Managing Boundaries

Quickly they [Oregon Benchmarks Initiative] realized that they could not deal with the state's economic future without dealing with its workforce, they could not deal with the workforce unless they dealt with education, they could not deal with education unless they dealt with kids and their families, and they could not deal with people unless they dealt with their health, their family cohesion, and their community.
   —Astrid Merget, 1994

Communicable diseases, environmentally induced illnesses, the consequences of alcoholism, and violent behavior affect all of us. They can only be addressed through effective collaborative relationships among all affected groups.
   —Doug Conrad and Steve Shortell, 1996

Management and governance structures must change to support the new forms of delivering health and medical services. The multidisciplinary provision of care across the continuum will not work if attempted within outmoded management and governance structures.
   —Steve Shortell et al., 1996

Thus far the argument has been advanced that in order to improve population health status, a balance of investments in various determinants and sectors is required. Whatever the appropriate investment balance is, it is possible that each determinant or sector (such as medical care, education, social services, or the environment) could achieve its maximum contribution in relative isolation from the others. It is also likely that a more integrated approach to population health would have advantages in terms of both cost and effectiveness through economies of scale and elimination of duplication. Furthermore, it could provide a more seamless interface for individuals, whose needs are now frequently unmet because of the fragmentation caused by various agents, funding streams, and bureaucratic structures.

The purpose of this chapter is to summarize the theoretical basis for integration or coordination across sectors, as well as to indicate previous and current attempts to manage boundaries across the determinants of health. Figure 38 illustrates these boundary issues in a Purchasing Population Health framework.

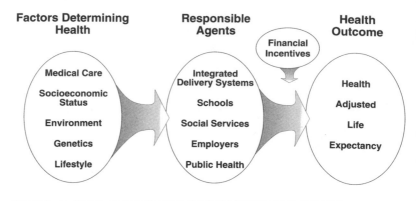

FIG. 38.   A model for improving population health.

On the left side are the factors that are known to impact on health, the determinants of health previously described. On the right is population health, measured in units of health adjusted life expectancy. Reaching this goal is achieved by agents, in the middle of the figure, that improve or maintain population health by their role in providing or enhancing the determinants of health. Determinants are not the responsibility of any particular agent. In terms of medical care, for example, the primary agent would be the health care sector; however, some medical care is the responsibility of the individual. Similarly, environmental determinants can be the responsibility of business, government, or the individual.

Acknowledging these relationships should help different agents understand both their own roles and responsibilities and those of other agents or social sectors. For example, even when health care providers acknowledge the role of nonmedical factors in producing health adjusted life expectancy, they often point out that their practices and organizations do not have responsibility for factors outside the medical care domain. It is important to recognize these boundaries and avoid incentives that do not take into account appropriate roles of different agents (providers, integrated systems, other social sectors, communities, the individual) in producing health. The boundaries are often unclear, and overlap across sectors is frequent.

The Case for Integration

Theory and experience in managing across boundaries where the product requires inputs from different sources or sectors are found primarily in the corporate world. Integration in business is usually thought of in two ways, horizontal or vertical.

Horizontal integration refers to the consolidation of like units of production, such as the merger of two small fast food restaurants or several large banks or corporations. The advantages are primarily those of economies of scale, where overhead expenses such as a physical plant, advertising, and knowledge of the business can be spread further to economic advantage.

Vertical integration, in contrast, refers to the coordination or linkage of different units or stages of the production process. It can be seen as the business arrangements that are used to control all aspects of the chain of production, including managing the supply of raw materials and services, as well as developing ready markets for the firm's products.

In the medical care sector, we are currently seeing both types of integration (Conrad and Shortell 1996). Examples of horizontal integration range from the merger of two small community hospitals to the creation of large national hospital chains, as seen in figure 39.

Some vertical integration is also taking place in this sector, as single organizations begin to consolidate clinics, hospitals, home care services, and even nursing homes, as illustrated in figure 40.

Such vertical integration is expected to have advantages in some spreading of management, physical, and information resources across these different sites, but in addition it potentially allows for closer coordination across these different components, resulting in seamless service and the elimination of wasteful overlap. This

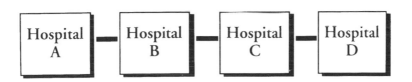

Horizontal integration. In healthcare, involves affiliation under one management umbrella of organizations that provide a similar level of care. Usually involves consolidation of resources among the organizations with the goals of increasing efficiency and taking advantage of economies of scale.

Hospital A — Hospital B — Hospital C — Hospital D

FIG. 39. Horizontal integration.
(From Conrad and Shortell 1996, *Frontiers of Health Services Management,* Fall 13 [1]: 7.)

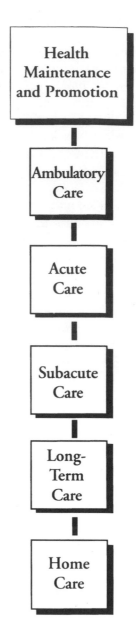

Vertical integration.
In healthcare, involves affiliation under one management umbrella of organizations that provide different levels of care. Goals include increasing efficiency, enhancing coordination of care along the continuum, and providing "one-stop shopping" for managed care purchasers and payers.

FIG. 40.   Vertical integration.
(From Conrad and Shortell 1996, *Frontiers of Health Services Management,*
Fall 13 [1]: 8.)

latter idea has the most relevance to Purchasing Population Health, in terms of the integration of the different determinants discussed in chapter 5.

It is easy to imagine how a degree of vertical integration might have benefits, such as the coordination between a hospital, clinic, and nursing home discussed earlier. But how are the limits of useful integration determined? This is critical since this discussion concerns broad determinants such as medical care, education, social services, and the environment. In addition to benefits, there can be inefficiencies in coordination across provider units of different types, particularly when some (such as education and environment) have multiple purposes, not all of which are directly related to the production of population health as it has been defined. As we saw previously, clean water has positive health benefits, but it also enhances our appreciation of natural beauty; the latter would not be considered a health benefit, although it would fall into the broader category of well-being. It is important to identify the limits beyond which vertical integration of broad components has disadvantages.

Lessons from Business

The theoretical foundations of vertical integration derive from work in industrial economics and strategic management. Early corporate examples in the steel and automobile industries demonstrated the advantages of ownership and control of all components of production. For example, in its early years the Ford Motor Company owned and operated every stage of production, from iron ore to finish and trim operations (except tires and glass). One reason for this strategy was that in the early development of the automobile, suppliers for such a risky new product were not available, and so Ford had no choice but to develop the components itself (Harrigan 1984).

Harrigan has also identified several characteristics of vertical integration that should be taken into consideration when examining these relationships. They include the following: how broad is the extent of integration, how much integration already exists within the organization through internal "sales" across different divisions or products, and the nature of coordination or ownership relationships that link related services.

Vertical integration theory originally supported a narrow controlling view based on market power and perfectly competitive industries, such as the Ford example given previously. It was often difficult to implement in practice, given the inflexible nature of such arrangements (i.e., needing to own and manage multiple production components) and the demands on management capabilities needed to reap the maximum benefit from such arrangements. These were some of the problems the vertically integrated auto industry had in meeting Japanese competition. This experience plus antitrust decisions created a tarnished image for traditional views of this strategy. Only recently have scholars such as Porter recognized the diversity of ways that vertical integration could be formed to make industries more competitive (Porter 1985).

More recently, the expansion of the vertical integration concept into more flexible arrangements such as the Value Added Partnership has been advocated, based on the view that computers and low-cost communication are tipping the competitive advantage back toward partnership of small companies, each of which performs one part of the value-added chain (Johnston and Lawrence 1988). Goldsmith has criticized certain aspects of traditional vertical integration in his concept of "virtual" integration (Goldsmith 1994), which favors coordination of different elements instead of ownership, but others have emphasized the difficulties in a virtual approach. Unfortunately, there is little empirical research that assesses costs, risks, and benefits of the different approaches to vertical integration. Most analysts emphasize the importance of the balance between cost control and flexibility and underscore the necessity of managerial and strategic attention to the balance and its implementation.

Lessons from Government

Similar issues and challenges are present in the field of public administration, both in theory and in practice. In some ways this is more complex, because the boundary issues are not only present across different public sector components but across public-private boundaries, to the extent that public sector organizations rely on private or not-for-profit firms to carry out components of their responsibility under contracts or grants.

Privatization
Some of these public sector considerations have been treated in the privatization debate, questioning which aspects of public services could be done more efficiently or effectively in the private sector. Much

of this discussion is ideological, but one particularly thoughtful analysis is that by John Donahue in his book *The Privatization Decision: Public Ends, Private Means* (Donahue 1989). In it he examines a number of public programs, including garbage collection, education, prisons, and defense, any one of which might be a candidate for either increased or totally private management. He develops a way of thinking about this decision from an effectiveness perspective and concludes that the nature of the program, and particularly the degree to which it has concrete objectives that can be measured and managed (garbage collection vs. defense research), is the critical element in such analysis.

Deregulation

In addition to these intrinsic issues, Kettl has recently argued in "Deregulating the Boundaries of Government: Would It Help?" that one of the reasons for reduced performance and responsiveness of government is that the boundaries have become far more numerous and complicated, so that almost all issues in areas as diverse as Medicare, highway construction, and job training have cross-agency ramifications (Kettl 1994). As a result, this complexity has grown faster than the ability to manage it. He states that

> shared responsibility for common problems, rather than more differentiated responsibility for separable problems, has come to define American politics. Where responsibility is shared, moreover, what matters most is what happens at the boundaries of responsibility: how federal, state and local governments balance their respective roles; how governments interact with their private and not-for-profit partners; and how these complex partnerships relate to citizens.

In the human service area, he notes that integration requires coordinating national goals with state and local initiatives managed typically through not-for-profit service providers.

State Examples

Astrid Merget, dean of the Maxwell School of Public Affairs at Syracuse University, has also commented that research in this area needs to be advanced to incorporate the long-term developmental nature of social change, the interrelatedness of problems, and joint production relationships (Merget 1994). She points out the example of the Oregon Benchmarks Initiative, in which three governors in succession have supported a process of integrated goals at the state level. The initiative initially was designed to deal with the state's economy in the year 2000, those involved realized that

they could not deal with the economic future without dealing with its workforce, that they could not deal with the workforce without dealing with education, that they could not deal with education unless they dealt with kids and their families, and they could not deal with people unless they dealt with their health, their family cohesion, and their community.

While many of these efforts can be implemented at the state level with public, private, and individual collaboration, many require federal partnership. Oregon has mapped out three clusters of activity (family stability, healthy children, and workforce development) in which they will look to federal flexibility in the form of waivers, commingling of funds, common definitions of eligibility, and simplified reporting.

Merget also cites the example coming out of the federal Department of Health and Human Services government "reinvention" exercise, which proposes that 140 discretionary programs for children and families from the Public Health Service and the Administration on Families and Children be consolidated into several age groupings, with bonus points for jurisdictions that wed the clusters together.

Federal Block Grants

The block grant process is not new and has had as one of its objectives allowing such integration and flexibility, with cost savings coming from funding authorization in broadly defined functional areas rather than in narrowly defined categories. President Nixon created three block grants in the mid-1970s: one for training and employment, one for housing and community development, and one for social services. Nine additional block grants were created in 1981 in areas such as health services, energy assistance, and mental health and substance abuse. A 1995 review of the federal block grant experience in the 1980s reported the following concerns and lessons for the future: since initial funding was based on prior categorical grant levels, block grant funding was not necessarily equitable; information for performance oversight was limited; flexibility was reduced as constraints were added over time; and there is a need for "a shift in focus of federal management and accountability toward program results, with correspondingly less emphasis on inputs and rigid adherence to rules" (U.S. General Accounting Office 1995).

We therefore can see that many integration initiatives outside of the health care sector have been undertaken; these may provide data about quality and efficiency advantages from vertically integrating across unlike factors in the production process. What about vertical integration in the health care arena?

Vertical Integration in Health Care and Health

With regard to health care itself, Conrad and Dowling indicate that the primary purposes of vertical integration are to enhance the comprehensiveness and continuity of patient care and to control the sources of patients and other users of a delivery system's services (Conrad and Dowling 1990). They state that one of the main lessons from the health maintenance organization (HMO) experience is the gain that comes in vertically structured arrangements as a result of using less expensive ambulatory services and implementing preventive treatment as opposed to relying on acute inpatient care. They also indicate that a large array of mechanisms exists both for administrative coordination at the interorganization or system level and at the clinical or patient care level. These are determined in part by the fit of the vertical integration strategy with the following set of considerations: the core missions of the organizations involved; capital requirements and financing; organizational management process, incentives, and accountability in support of integration; the amount, type, and extent of resources needed to carry out the integration strategy; and the need to broaden both clinical and managerial perspectives on case-mix management and quality assurance.

Fit with Mission

The first consideration, that of fit with mission, comes close to organizing for population health, since by definition it requires some linking of a patient population with the breadth of services and interventions related to the determinants of health explored earlier.

Whereas a theoretical model and empirical research for the optimal extent and type of integration and the boundary interfaces are missing, there appears to be a resurgence of belief and experimentation that allege that less fragmentation will increase the efficiency and quality of the health adjusted life expectancy production function. To a considerable degree, one can expect systems of care that become more vertically and horizontally integrated to be able to find the economies of scale and reduced costs of contracting that bundling and integration allow. Such arrangements should also permit more seamless and patient-centered care, which is now often interrupted by boundaries and gaps between organizations and financing mechanisms providing individual components of service.

One way to think of this is to consider the difficulties encountered between the hospital, outpatient clinic or doctor's office, and nursing home or home care agency in the care of a single elderly patient. While there will always be some difficulty in such interfaces, the fact that services are provided by different organizations and across many funding streams and bureaucracies increases the difficulties significantly. Ideally, the patient would receive bundled and coordinated interventions or a program of services for the condition.

Examples of Vertical Integration in U.S. Health Care

There are multiple examples of past or current efforts to devise new organizational forms across boundaries of both medical care and population health that illustrate the possibilities of extending this concept further in the pursuit of Purchasing Population Health.

OEO Neighborhood Health Centers

An early experiment in the United States was that of the health programs of the federal Office of Economic Opportunity (OEO), launched in the 1960s as a part of the Kennedy/Johnson War on Poverty. The health component of this effort was the establishment of a large number of community health centers, largely in impoverished neighborhoods in inner cities and rural areas (Reynolds 1976). Although mainly devoted to primary care services, these centers had an active outreach component through neighborhood or family health workers who were from the community and whose job it was to link the center and the community it served.

These centers embodied the population health concept in that the whole population and catchment area were their responsibility and the health status of those who were not regular users of the clinic was as important as those who were. The health teams were composed of physicians, nurse-practitioners, midwives, pharmacists, and family health workers, who brought an integrating dimension to medical care. In addition, the OEO program recognized the broader determinants of health, and so centers had housing, job training, school health, and legal advocacy components. While the ambulatory care core of many of these centers remains today, the broader population health components gradually disappeared as the grant program dwindled over time. This experience stands as a clear example of what happens when a sound concept is not embedded in enduring organizational and financial mechanisms.

Health Maintenance Organizations

It has already been mentioned that health maintenance organizations (HMOs) are one of the best examples of vertical integration in medical care delivery. Their origins derived from the desire of employers to contract with a single organization for prepaid care for a population of workers. Most such organizations have been variations on linkages between hospitals and medical groups. The fundamental economic principle of prepayment has been a strong incentive for HMOs to find economies in substituting ambulatory care for inpatient care and for controlling the use of physician specialists. An additional goal was better coordination of services from the patient perspective. While prevention ("health maintenance") was philosophically embraced by HMOs, this emphasis has not necessarily translated into common practice, both because the economies of prevention have not been fully established so that this expense could be justified and because outcomes have not been explicitly rewarded. Furthermore, HMOs remain largely in the medical care field, since there are no incentives at all for a broader product. However, the integration of doctors and hospitals into managed care systems stimulated by the capitation financial incentive was and continues today to develop as the most powerful example of vertical integration in health care, and at the least suggests further opportunities for cost-effectiveness if financial incentives were applied to a broader product definition such as population health.

Integrated Delivery Systems

At the current time, the quest for cost savings in medical care has stimulated the almost frantic development of a large variety of integrated delivery systems at regional or national levels. These organizations are less structured than the early HMOs but are growing very rapidly. Every month new vertical and virtual arrangements are developed, which makes keeping current with them a task in itself. While some of these systems are integrating some broader aspects of medical care such as home health, at this point most of these efforts are still focused on the integration of hospital and physician components (Shortell and Hull 1996). As these systems enroll larger populations and the market share stabilizes over the next five years, they will form a population basis for further vertical integration of the additional determinants of health if appropriate broad incentives are developed and implemented. These developing structures unifying large populations provide a unique opportunity in the United States to make significant progress on these challenges of integration without having to start from the beginning as may be the case elsewhere. However, significant barriers remain in the areas of resources, organizational culture, incentives, management and governance systems, as well as the legal and regulatory environment (Conrad and Shortell 1996).

Social Health Maintenance Organizations (SHMOs)

The best current operational example in the United States of vertical integration beyond hospital and physician services is that of the Medicare SHMO demonstrations. The idea behind this was that economies and service benefits similar to those found by HMOs in acute care could also be expanded if elements of long-term and community care were incorporated into the risk package for the elderly. The four SHMOs still in existence serve 22,000 Medicare beneficiaries with standard Medicare hospital and physician services but also include prescription drugs and up to $1,000 per month of community long-term care and short-term nursing home service. While methodological difficulties have precluded definitive assessment of cost and outcomes in comparison to fee-for-service alternatives, many observers believe that such demonstrations have shown the way for the benefits that integration across providers can yield in both dimensions. The current waivers are due to end in 1997, but there is activity in Congress to extend these waivers and possibly to begin up to seven new sites. It will be important to track this experience carefully because it is still the broadest relevant U.S. experience, even if it is only in the medical care sector (Rivlin and Weiner 1988; Harrington, Newcomer, and Preston 1993).

Current Efforts

Even though nothing as broad as the OEO idea currently exists in the United States, major organizations and researchers have outlined possible approaches. Many of these were developed in the cauldron of national thinking about health reform in the 1992–94 period. Shortell advanced the general proposal for health promotion accountability regions (HPARs), in which integrated delivery systems at the state or regional level would be reimbursed for health status improvement (Shortell 1992). Both the American Hospital Association and the Catholic Hospital Association developed proposals for national health reform that envisioned a broader goal of community health and vertical integration beyond physicians and hospitals (AHA 1993; CHA 1992). The Healthcare Forum, the former Western Hospital Association, has championed the Healthy Communities movement, which focuses on prevention and health promotion at the community level. This latter effort has strong ties to the global Healthy Communities effort of the World Health Organization.

The National Community Care Network Demonstration program, jointly sponsored by the American Hospital Association, the Catholic Hospital Association, and the Voluntary Hospital Association, is currently working with a number of communities that have joined together to advance a system of coordinated health and human services (AHA 1995). The Catholic Health Association has published a *Handbook for Planning and Developing Integrated Delivery,* which presents their approach and vision for a healthier United States (CHA 1995).

Figure 41 highlights the required transition from "old thinking" to "new thinking," described as a new mind-set of collaboration focused on community health, seamless continuum of care, management within fixed resources, and community accountability.

All of these beginning efforts are evidence of scholarly and organizational interest in the idea of greater vertical integration of the determinants of health for the purpose of producing population health, showing an inclination and willingness to act to achieve this goal. However, at least in the United States, the frantic race for market share, cost containment, and profits has relegated these efforts to the sidelines. Unfortunately, the turbulence is so great that many equate change with progress, depending on what the definition of progress is, which may or may not be the case.

Vertical Integration in Other Countries

Joint Commissioning in Great Britain

The concept of vertical integration between health and social services has recently been implemented in Great Britain as a part of the National Health Service (NHS) and Community Care reforms of the Thatcher period. A large number of changes have taken place in each sector, with general movement toward a purchaser-provider separation and a "mixed economy" or quasi-market approach to public provision and contracting with the private sector that has been extensively documented by Gerald Wistow and his colleagues at the Nuffield Institute in Leeds (Wistow 1982; Wistow et al. 1994). Regional health authorities

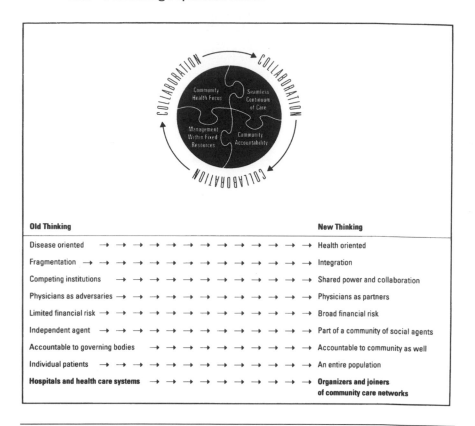

FIG. 41.   Community care network strategies.
(From *Transforming Health Care Delivery: Toward Community Care Networks.*
Reprinted with permission of the American Hospital Association, Copyright © 1993.)

were separated from hospitals and began to use competitive principles for purchasing some services. In physician services, the development of partial capitation, "GP fundholding," allowed general practitioners to purchase certain services such as elements of nursing and home care from the private sector instead of from traditional public agencies (Dixon and Glennerster 1995; Mays and Dixon 1996). In addition, community care reforms shifted certain social services out of hospital budgets and into the social care sector under the control of local authorities (Wistow 1995a,b). The latter seems to be motivated significantly by the need to reduce health spending and to transfer certain services from an entitlement sector (the NHS) to a means-tested sector (Community Care).

Previous academic and demonstration efforts have looked at the integration of community care and health care services in Great Britain. The most notable was the work of Challis and colleagues in Kent on demonstrating cost-effectiveness in integrated approaches to long-term home care for frail elderly with frontline social service staff (Challis and Davies 1986). More recently, the idea of joint commissioning has been developed, with some movement to consolidate health authorities and local authorities to potentially allow for integration and resource transfer across sectors.

Canadian Efforts

There has been considerable recent discussion and policy analysis in Canada about the issues of "devolution" of funding and authority for health and social services from the national to the provincial and subprovincial levels. During the 1980s, every province produced proposed policies through task forces and commissions, which had a central theme of devolving authority for the purposes of cost containment, health outcome improvement, and service responsiveness through integration and coordination of services. In this case, devolution and decentralization were seen as instruments to an end rather than an end in themselves. By 1996, 123 devolved authorities in health care had emerged, with a range in population from 7,000 to more than one million (Lomas, Woods, and Veenstra 1996). The only province not included is Ontario. It is too early to determine the effectiveness of such programs, but evaluations are under way. In general, all are responsible for local planning, priority setting, allocation of funds, and managing services for greater effectiveness within the constraints of provincially defined broad core services. Funding is from the province, primarily based on historical flows but at reduced levels. An interesting exception is Saskatchewan, where funding is based on a per capita need formula.

Regarding broader vertical integration across different sectors, the situation in Prince Edward Island is most relevant. In October 1993, the provincial government initiated a Health and Community Services Act to "implement the Partnership in Better Health Report on reforming the provincial system of health, public housing, probation and corrections, income security, child welfare, and other social services." It derived its strategy from 10 principles that included a recognition of the broad determinants of health, the need to integrate health with economic and social development, and regional resource allocation strategies. Five regional authorities were created to consolidate the previous categorical budgets and to reallocate at their discretion, constrained by the requirement to deliver a core program. Each region can use surpluses for any priorities it deems appropriate but must also cover any deficits itself (Youens 1996). Again, it is too early to draw any conclusions from this experiment, but Lomas and colleagues have identified some early lessons to consider: avoid linking reallocation with resource reductions, deal early on with cross-sector labor issues, and provide much better education and preparation to deal with professional and public resistance (Lomas, Rachlis, and Kumar 1996).

Swedish Cabinet Ministers Committee

In Sweden, a public health committee of cabinet ministers has recently been formed, chaired by the minister of health and social affairs, which will include the ministers of education and research, labor, housing, agriculture, and finance. The key motive is the need for a strong equity-oriented coordinated intersectorial health (not health care) policy (Swedish Ministry of Health and Social Affairs 1995).

Integration across Public and Private Sectors

The preceding examples of vertical integration in the production of health primarily relate either to the private sector (e.g., HMOs) or the public sector (e.g., the Prince Edward Island experiment). Contractual relationships may cross this boundary, primarily from the public sector to the private sector and primarily when the public sector agent is a purchaser rather than a provider of direct services (e.g., Medicare capitation contracts or independent community care contractors in Great Britain).

In the U.S. context, the challenge is to move to more complete vertical integration across the components of medical care, from prevention to acute care to long-term care. This can be done in the private sector, as with the HMO sites, or in public sector activities, such as in the Veterans Administration, the Department of Defense, or the Indian Health Service health care systems. It is critical to design financial incentives to foster integration within such sectors.

As stated earlier, major aspects of population health improvement will come from balanced investments in other sectors, as shown in the agent column of figure 38. Whereas in the United States most of the provision and much of the financing of medical care are in the private sector, many of the other determinants such as education and social services are predominantly in the public sector. Other determinants, such as environmental factors, income distribution, and community social cohesion, are mixed in both public and private sectors.

While anticipated in the work of the 1928–32 Committee on the Costs of Medical Care (Sigmond 1995), it is not easy to conceive of models that allow for vertical integration across public and private sectors. Almost certainly in the United States the relationships would not be of ownership forms of integration, where all of these entities are controlled in either the public or private sectors. It is more likely that some coordinated form of virtual integration will need to be developed, with those relationships organized at community, state, or regional levels. Without such relationships, and with a single broad measure of health outcome such as health adjusted life expectancy, it would not be fair to reward or penalize one sector for the achievements or failures of another.

Shortell and colleagues have recently continued to provide leadership in this area with their new book *Remaking Health Care in America* (Shortell et al. 1996). In it they outline their vision of a "community health care management system," which is the fourth stage of system maturation that will "begin to focus on community-wide health care needs through alliances, coalitions, linkages, and partnerships with public health and community and social service agencies." This begins with a community needs assessment that "projects the needs of different groups and converts these into likely utilization of health care services and resources." They use the term *organized* delivery system rather than *integrated* delivery system throughout the book, since they believe that "integration is an end state that few, if any, current systems have achieved." They indicate the critical role that virtual organizations across the community will have to play, and the critical integrative function for information systems to "incorporate community and public health data and to link one organized delivery system's data with another's." Their book describes the experience that 11 organized delivery systems across the United States have had in beginning down this path.

In order to support such integration across sectors, much additional cost-effectiveness research is needed for all of the non–health care determinants. As much criticism as medical care receives, the studies of cost-effectiveness of various interventions and programs are much more advanced in the health arena than in other sectors. Drummond and Stoddart have recently called for such a cross-sectoral framework for health status cost-effectiveness analysis, but almost no work exists in this field at this time (Drummond and Stoddart 1995). The work presented at the end of chapter 6 (table 15) on the evidence for 500 lifesaving interventions crossing several sectors (Tengs et al. 1995) from a risk analytic perspective should be expanded into other determinants of population health.

Incentives for Integration across Sectors

For virtual or coordinated integration to work, there still needs to be a locus of responsibility or authority calling for cross-sectoral results. Currently there is no entity or market force driving the cross-sectoral outcome of population health. It is appropriate to expect private sector health care organizations with powerful political and community standing to use their community and political influence to indirectly impact on appropriate health enhancing investments in other sectors (environment, education, social services, public health), which will accrue to their population's health status improvement as well as to that of the community at large.

Voluntary efforts, however, are unlikely to be effective in themselves or in all communities or regions. It will probably be necessary in a later stage to develop some form of public-private or governmental mechanism to provide the framework and clout for integration across sectors, and one, the Health Outcomes Trust, will be proposed in chapter 9. When it comes to the bottom line of resource reallocation, resistance from affected professional groups and established economic interests will be strong. Advocacy for some of the determinants of health such as education and social services historically is weak in comparison to medical interests, for example. Such a mechanism may seem contrary to the opening promise of no new massive bureaucracy, but it is envisioned to be primarily local and primarily a virtual or coordination effort. It was suggested earlier that public health agencies, freed of their personal medical care responsibilities, could possibly take the lead in such coordination at the state and local levels. It is important to look at state and regional examples where some types of similar integration may provide ideas for organizational arrangements for Purchasing Population Health in the future.

Can We Learn from Environmental Policy?

One sector that may provide some guidance is that of environmental improvement. In some ways this sector has been ahead in the establishment of standards for outcomes such as levels of air and water pollution. It has also begun to include some of the costs of environmental disposal in the prices of products, creating incentives for a long-term view of environmental outcomes and protection. In addition, it has required public-private interaction, if not collaboration or integration. Particular progress has been noted in the Netherlands, where serious environmental challenges led to their National Environmental Policy Plan, more commonly known as the Green Plan (Johnson 1995). A major collaborative effort of government and industry, it is successfully weaving together complex systems such as water, soil, air, and energy in the context of economics, health, and carrying capacity. It has benefited from the development of innovative planning processes, such as planning models that allow 40–50 year horizons for identifying actions needed now in order to create sustainable economics and technology in the future. So far, it appears to have successfully integrated business into public plans through signed agreements, allowing industry representatives to determine the most efficient ways of reaching the goals, rather than having the mechanisms dictated to them by government. Such processes have fostered considerable progress, which has elsewhere been stymied by regulation and legal battles.

It is likely that we will have to look beyond health care to other sectors such as the environment for examples of integration, particularly across public-private boundaries, in order to achieve the promise of Purchasing Population Health.

Of course, there always remains the issue of where the boundaries of health end, returning us to the definitional issues between health and wellness covered in chapter 4. Some futurists attempt to integrate all of human activity in their thinking, so that Hazel Henderson highlights global country futures indicators (Henderson 1991) and Ilona Kickbush talks of governmental Departments of Consequences, with responsibility for integrating across many sectors, not dissimilar to but even broader than the Swedish Cabinet Council discussed earlier (Kickbush 1994). For 10 years, the Institute for Innovation in Social Policy at Fordham has issued its annual Index of Social Health, which "monitors the social well-being of the nation" (Fordham Institute 1996). While many of these arguments apply to very broad views of social outcomes, the thinking is also useful as we consider the narrower challenges in improving the quantity and quality of life.

Summary

This chapter has identified both the opportunities and the challenges in vertical integration across boundaries of population health determinants. Efficient and effective population health purchasing will require not only the determination of relative cost-effectiveness as discussed in chapter 6 but some mechanism for coordination and integration as discussed here. **We should immediately get on with the task of broadening vertical integration across medical determinants (long-term care, public health), while developing models and demonstration projects for linking nonmedical determinants.** Chapter 9 will deal with some of the practical issues and possibilities in implementing such a framework. But before we proceed to implementation, chapter 8 will consider some of the distributional and ethical issues in different populations that are critical in a Purchasing Population Health approach that aligns health resources to health outcomes.

8 · Different Populations, Different Needs?

In the presence of scarcity, resources devoted to the health
care of one person may be denied some other person who
might have benefited from them.
　—Alan Williams, 1996

A need for health care is the minimum amount of resources
required to exhaust a person's capacity to benefit.
　—Tony Culyer, 1995

The previous chapters developed the argument for a single measure of
population health, such as health adjusted life expectancy (HALE), as
the basis for providing financial incentives to providers at a community
or health plan level. Such an aggregate measure would help consumers
and purchasers judge the relative cost and quality of alternative plans. It
would not replace the utility of multiple disease-specific measures at
smaller program levels but would become a single standard of comparability such as the gross domestic product or the Consumer Price
Index.

Figure 24 indicated that the goal of Purchasing Population
Health was to move both of the population HALE components upward,
increasing life expectancy as well as the number of years spent at greater
quality of health. The following three components were depicted in
table 11 as composing the Years of Healthy Life measure, one possible
HALE measurement tool:

· Mortality: expected years of life remaining
· Disability: activity limitation
· Health Perception: self-perceived health status

Components two and three are used to adjust the life years or
mortality component to produce HALE, which would become the purchasing standard. Overall improvement in population HALEs would
become the most important indicator both for the absolute level of
health outcomes and for comparing the relative progress between communities or plans.

As stated in chapter 6, this is a utilitarian perspective that
places value on better health outcomes for the resources expended. But
is such a HALE basis for efficient purchasing equitable or fair for all
members of the population? Is the absolute level of HALE improvement

a valid basis for judging progress toward outcome? Should any two health systems or communities with the same total HALE increases per person be rewarded exactly the same? Are there additional issues of HALE distribution and equity across populations that should be taken into consideration? The rationing argument in chapter 6 focused on overall cost-effectiveness but did not deal with subpopulation issues. These require further discussion and consideration before moving on to the final chapters regarding administrative implementation of Purchasing Population Health.

No Two Populations Are Alike

If the population were divided neatly into groups of similar size, age structure, and mortality/morbidity profiles, resource equity would be relatively straightforward. But people live in communities of different socioeconomic, environmental, or disease susceptibility characteristics, and populations can be "naturally" healthier due to geography, income, age structure, and culture and perhaps also as a result of religious beliefs that lead to good health habits. People also choose or are assigned to a large variety of fee-for-service or managed care health care delivery systems.

In addition, it is possible for health plans to intentionally create a healthier patient panel by actively encouraging membership of healthy individuals through marketing in health clubs and certain geographic areas or "demarketing" in areas with many older or poorer people. This is known as "favorable selection" or "cream skimming." All these inequalities have to be taken into account in any purchasing framework that provides incentives for higher HALE levels. In other words, market competition based on outcomes should operate from a "level playing field" instead of from accidental or intentional different underlying population health status or potential for improvement.

Quite a bit is known about how populations of different characteristics vary both in the level of health and in terms of the underlying factors responsible for these differences. Clyde Hertzman and colleagues at the University of British Columbia have highlighted this concept of "Heterogeneities in Health Status," which they define as "differences in aggregate measures of population health status between or among population groups which are consistently associated with some defining characteristic of this group" (Hertzman, Frank, and Evans 1994). Some of these differences have already been seen as they relate to

TABLE 17.   Factors in Population Heterogeneity

Life Cycle Stages	Population Characteristics
1. Perinatal (0–1)	1. Socioeconomic status
2. "Misadventure" (1–44)	2. Gender
3. Chronic disease (45–74)	3. Ethnicity
4. Senescence (75+)	4. Geography

Source: Adapted with permission from Evans, Robert G., et al. (eds.) *Why Are Some People Healthy and Others Not? The Determinants of Health of Populations.* (New York: Aldine de Gruyter) Copyright © 1994 Walter de Gruyter, Inc., New York.

mortality rates by gender or race. Hertzman and coworkers suggest the factors shown in table 17 and others as important in thinking about population differences in health status.

These can obviously be combined with each other to create multiple levels of population difference that in turn are influenced by factors such as genetics, differential susceptibility, lifestyle, physical environment, social environment, and access to care.

Is Purchasing Population Health Fair?

In the last decade, a considerable body of scholarship by philosophers, ethicists, physicians, and economists has analyzed the distributional and ethical issues of focusing on health care outcomes in a health adjusted life expectancy framework. In general, much of the concern questions whether such a formula-driven outcome would lead to inequitable results. These commentators have pointed out that different categories of injustice could result from a "QALY egalitarianism" framework in which all QALYs* are presumed to be equal. Alan Williams takes this position as a working hypothesis "in order to get the work [of research and analysis] done," while at the same time doing empirical work on how QALYs might have different values for different groups of individuals (Williams 1988, 1992).

---

*Much distributional health ethics writing is European and focuses on the specific HALE measure "quality adjusted life years (QALY)"; this term will be used generically in this chapter.

This chapter addresses the following questions of subpopulation distribution and ethics:

- How can "need" for health in different populations be determined? Should improvement in initially less healthy populations be given greater value or reward?
- Should other "social values" (such as having dependents) be given higher priority in determining targets for population health improvement?
- Does the HALE measurement system discriminate against the disabled? Should incentives be used to compensate for previous poor health from disability or other causes?
- Does a HALE measurement system discriminate against the elderly?
- Does it matter if a few persons get the most benefit, or should improvement be more equitably distributed among all individuals in the community or plan?
- Is the level of utilization or access to health services a relevant consideration?
- How can we realistically address such ethical and distributional concerns?

These are issues of considerable importance as well as potential controversy and deserve significant attention in the phase 1 "debate, research, and demonstration" period in the next five years.

Determining Need for Health

Do different health plans and communities have different initial levels of health and "need" for health resources? How can "need" for health in different populations be determined? Should improvement in initially less healthy populations be given greater incentive or reward?

The issue of "need" for health outcome improvement relates to population heterogeneity because each unique population has a different initial baseline level of health status or HALEs. Whatever the reason for these differences, it is important to consider what the potential for improvement is either from additional medical services or from other determinants of health. To use an extreme example to make the point clear, if poor population health status were due totally to individuals with a genetic disease that could not be altered, or to a community trapped in a poisonous environment that could not be improved, how strong would the rationale be for clinical or environmental resource allocation to these groups?

The concept of "need" appears simple initially but quickly becomes complicated. Many analysts avoid this concept because of definitional difficulties and the prevailing economic framework of "demand" coming from a supply and demand perspective. In such a framework, if someone "needs" something, he or she will express this desire by purchasing in the marketplace the item that is needed, and, as a consequence, supply will increase. While such a framework has some usefulness in thinking about health services and health, we have shown before that it has limitations since the consumer does not have complete information about the product and its effectiveness and often someone else does the demanding (health professionals). In addition, a third party such as an insurance company, a company benefit manager, or a federal or state government (in the case of Medicare or Medicaid or in private insurance or managed care organizations) is often the purchaser on the individual's behalf. Indeed, in the interests of cost containment, requests for medical care that the patient and/or the physician feel are "needed" are sometimes denied altogether.

Need as "Capacity to Benefit"

Williams and Culyer have championed an alternative concept of need at the University of York that they term *capacity to benefit* (Williams 1974; Culyer 1993; Williams 1997b). In addition to going beyond supply and demand, this concept also goes beyond the perspective of initial baseline level of health, because, as indicated earlier, unhealthy individuals and populations cannot be said to need more resources for medical care or other investment without regard to their potential for improving their health status. In addition, capacity to benefit rules out programs and interventions that might be desired by individuals or providers but that do not make a positive contribution to health adjusted life expectancy. One crude measure of capacity to benefit might be the premature mortality measure mentioned in chapter 4, table 6; this, however arbitrarily, gives no value to living beyond age 65 and only considers length of life as benefit.

As shown previously in table 12 (chap. 5), the Centers for Disease Control and Prevention (CDCP) have indicated that 50 percent of the annual deaths in the United States result primarily from nongenetic factors. Subpopulations that have overall higher levels of preventable factors or different patterns of cause of death either have a different

TABLE 18.   Hypothetical Communities of Different Initial Health Status

	U.S. Population	Average Health Community	Less Healthy (−20%)	More Healthy (+20%)
Population	250 million	250,000	250,000	250,000
Life years	12.4 billion	12.4 million	9.9 million	14.8 million
YHLs	11.1 billion	11.1 million	8.9 million	13.3 million

capacity to benefit potential or require different types of investment to improve health outcomes. Whereas this is the type of information that is needed, the CDCP conditions are limited only to mortality and do not include quality of life considerations as HALEs do. As Purchasing Population Health becomes more sophisticated and incentives develop from a capacity to benefit framework, it will be necessary to assess and address the cause-specific factors responsible for different baseline levels of HALEs in subpopulations.

"Natural" examples include disproportionate numbers of persons with AIDS, low-birth-weight babies, and cancers from a local environmental cause; "artificial" examples such as "cream skimming" have been discussed previously. Fielding has coined the term *ameliorability quotient* to refer to a specific way to measure capacity to benefit; it must be remembered that amelioration can come both from medical care and/or from socioeconomic improvement (Fielding 1995). Identification of medical as well as social ameliorability quotients for different subpopulations would serve as a guide for incentive strategies for an appropriate investment balance.

Table 18 presents a hypothetical example (using data from fig. 24) that should help frame the issue regarding populations of differing initial health status.

In this example the healthier (for whatever reason) health plan or community begins with 2.2 million more YHLs than the average (which has 11.1 million) and 4.4 million more than the less healthy one, for the same size population. Should Purchasing Population Health reward improvements in each community or health plan equally, recognizing that they have different initial levels of health? What incentive options exist for equitable progress for improving population health where different initial health status or capacity to benefit exists? Figures 42 and 43 illustrate alternative ways of thinking about this, using the hypothetical data on three populations from table 18.

Population A is initially more healthy, with 13.3 million HALEs, while population B is less healthy, with 8.9 million. Both have

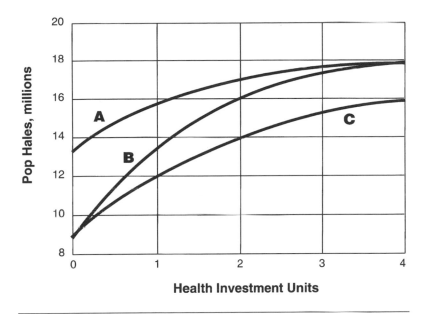

FIG. 42. Health improvement: different initial level, different capacity to benefit.

the same capacity to benefit, potentially able to reach 17.9 million HALEs after an investment of four units of health-promoting resources. Population C begins as less healthy but only has the capacity to reach 15.9 HALEs after a similar resource investment.

Figure 43 shows the same data from a marginal improvement perspective; the vertical axis is the change in HALEs gained per unit of resources expended.

All show diminishing marginal return, with less increase in output for each extra unit of added resource. But population B has the greatest marginal return, followed by C and then A; A has the least because it starts at the highest point and has therefore the least capacity to benefit. Of course, these are only three of many possibilities that exist.

Who Gets Priority?

There are several options for differential resource allocation in such a situation. Taking A and B, for example, one choice might be to invest all available resources in B to bring it up to the level of A (13.3 HALEs) and then invest additional resources equally between the two populations so that they approach the maximum of 17.9 together (in parallel). This would reflect a value judgment that the worst off in society should

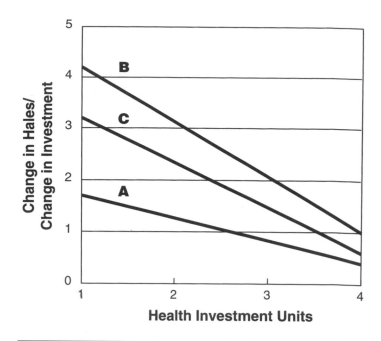

FIG. 43. Marginal health improvement: different initial need, different capacity to benefit.

receive priority, a position labeled "maximin" by philosopher John Rawls (Rawls 1971; Daniels 1985).

On the other hand, some might advocate providing resources to make some improvement in all populations from the beginning; it would be possible to invest proportionally in A and B in relation to their marginal return curves, so that for each 1 unit invested in B, about 0.4 unit would be invested in A. This would move each population gradually toward optimal health status in parallel from the beginning. Again, combinations of these two approaches are possible as well. The point of these figures is to illustrate that a rational approach to alternative investment decisions is possible when initial level of health status and capacity to benefit are established. This counters the argument that a QALY approach to resource distribution cannot incorporate different purchaser or community value perspectives. We will return to mechanisms for considering such alternatives later in this chapter and in chapter 9.

A change in the policies for the allocation of scarce organs for transplantation has recently been debated in the United States when it was proposed that persons with chronic liver disease be put in the "second tier" of recipients after those with better long-term survival prospects i.e. capacity to benefit (*USA Today* 1996; Steinbrook 1997).

> **This is one of the first times that the concept of relative benefit has been used as a possible criterion for allocation decisions, and while the outcome of this debate has not yet been determined, the fact that such considerations are beginning to enter into policy discussion is important in its own right and signals that such considerations will become more explicit in the future.**

Many subpopulation equity considerations have focused on distribution issues such as income and race (in economics, the term *equity* is often only applied to issues of differential income). Culyer (1988) and Culyer and Wagstaff (1993) argue convincingly that if what is being distributed is viewed from a need or capacity to benefit framework, then the disadvantage conferred by a population having a higher level of low-income persons or groups with higher genetic susceptibility, for example, is already reflected in this greater need or capacity to benefit, and therefore additional consideration based on such factors as income or race would not be necessary and would in fact be double counting. Understanding the reason (the "ameliorability quotient" mentioned previously) for a higher capacity to benefit might aid in determining the best remedy. However, it does not argue for additional incentives other than what are already embodied in differential capacity to benefit, unless these factors are deemed to have extra social value (see the following). It is certainly possible that a purchasing health outcomes approach might stimulate investment in communities or health plans with current lower levels of investment, since units of health improvement in underserved populations may be purchased more cheaply at the most cost-effective part of the health production function. This of course assumes that all these populations have basic health insurance coverage and that the health production function curves for all populations follow the general shape of the curves drawn in figure 43.

Discrimination against the Disabled?

Would HALE measurement discriminate against the disabled? Should incentives be used to compensate for previous poor health from disability or other causes? This reflects the concern that the use of HALEs or QALYs for health care allocation would lead to "double jeopardy," in which someone with a disability is doubly disadvantaged since his or her disability might give that individual a lower initial QALY value (reflecting the fact that all of this person's life years may be at a lower level of quality than those of a nondisabled person) and therefore would be systematically discriminated against in treatment decisions (Singer et al. 1995). This is not a hypothetical argument, since one of the legal challenges to the initial Oregon Plan was filed by disability advocates. This concern can be countered, however, by the realization that a HALE incentive framework is forward looking in terms of improvement and does not initially at least deal with "compensatory justice" that gives additional consideration for the lack of quality of life previously suffered by the disabled person. Instead of looking back, HALE maximization would direct resources to those where the greatest outcome gains could be expected, which would not necessarily be those with the highest levels at the end of treatment.

An Example

Assume two 40 year olds with 30 years of life remaining, the disabled person having those years at 80 percent quality and the nondisabled at 90 percent. The disabled person has 24 QALYs remaining (30 at 80 percent) and the nondisabled 27 (30 at 90 percent). If a hip replacement or treatment of depression or an increase in air quality adds 2 percent to each one's quality factor, both persons will add 0.6 QALYs (30 years × .02) to their lives. The investment choice is equal, even though the disabled person will still have fewer QALYs in his or her whole life (24.6 vs. 27.6).

Discrimination against the Elderly?

Do HALE incentives discriminate against old persons? This concern has received the most ethical attention (Harris 1987, 1988; Lockwood 1988). It asserts that since HALEs are the product of life years and quality of those years, it follows that treatments or other health promoting investments will automatically favor younger persons, who by definition have more life years to gain, and that this fact will overwhelm any quality factor for older ages.

Three Examples

In a very simple example, assume that a 5 year old and a 65 year old both have acquired bacterial pneumonia, which will result in death if untreated but which could be completely cured with treatment. The cost of antibiotic medication is the same for both persons. For the same invest-ment, the young person will gain about 75 QALYs (75 years at a quality of one) while the older person will gain about 15 QALYs (15 years at a quality of one). If a choice had to be made about these two investments, the argument goes, the younger person would always be favored.

In such a simple scenario, this conclusion is correct and per-haps meritorious. But consider a more complex (and controversial) sce-nario: experimental chemotherapy for a 20 year old with AIDS and a hip replacement for a 45 year old, both of equal cost. Hypothetically, the 20 year old might gain 10 extra life years at 10 percent better quality (1.0 QALYs), while the 45 year old might gain no life years, but the 35 remaining would have a 5 percent better quality (1.75 QALYs gained). If a choice had to be made on QALY cost-effectiveness, the older person would be favored. It is fair to conclude that a HALE (or QALY) outcome incentive does not always favor the young over the old, although invest-ments producing healthier lives for young persons with longer to live would often be favored by HALE methodology in a world of constrained resources. However, such a basic framework does not seem intrinsically unfair as a starting point.

On the other hand, it would be possible to reward differentially by age, if it were decided that either younger or older persons deserved a higher valuation than need alone would confer (for example, society might weight older persons higher due to their experience and wisdom that society needs). To illustrate this point, table 19 gives another hypo-thetical example, based on age groups, again using data derived from figure 24.

The data in the second column is for the same average healthy community presented previously, with 250,000 population and a total of 11.1 million years of healthy life. The third column shows a 5 percent overall increase to 11,658 and demonstrates how this would be dis-tributed if each age group had the identical 5 percent increase. The last column shows how the same 5 percent total increase to 11,658 could be achieved by targeting different age segments of the population. In this example, the 10 to 39 year old age group shows a 10 percent increase (perhaps from lowered alcohol-related traffic accidents or lower AIDS death rates) and the over 70 group a 15 percent increase (perhaps from lower stroke mortality or better quality of life from hip replacement or treatment of depression). But the other two age groups have decreases in their YHLs, perhaps because of increased infant mortality in the youn-ger age group and higher death rates from cervical and breast cancer in the middle age group.

TABLE 19. Differential Health Outline Improvement by Age Group

Age Group	Years of Healthy Life (millions)		
	Average Healthy Community	5% Increase at Each Age	Variable 5% Increase
<10	2,626	2,757 (5%)	2,571 (−5%)
10–39	6,230	6,542 (5%)	6,853 (10%)
40–69	2,050	2,153 (5%)	2,007 (−2%)
70+	196	6 (5%)	225 (15%)
Total	11,102	11,658 (5%)	11,658 (5%)

Because the QALY concept was developed primarily to consider the relative cost and outcome of individual treatment decisions (as in the example in chap. 4, fig. 22, drug treatment vs. surgery for coronary artery disease), it highlights the impact on individuals and raises the specter of resource choices between one specific old person and one specific child. However, HALE improvement incentives would operate at a much more aggregate health plan or community level (see fig. 45, chap. 9), leaving clinicians considerable freedom for choice in terms of individual patient treatment. Of course, it is still appropriate to be alert to any systematic age or other bias resulting from implicit or explicit purchasing strategies.

Williams has recently developed a "fair innings" argument, in which he argues that age is one appropriate criterion for choosing people who could benefit from health care. "So I am encouraged to hope that, in the interests of fairness between the generations, the members of my generation will exercise restraint in the demands we make on the health care system. We should not object to age being one of the criteria (though not the sole criterion) used in the prioritisation of health care, even though it will disadvantage us. The alternative is too outrageous to contemplate—namely, that we expect the young to make large sacrifices so that we can enjoy small benefits. That would not be fair" (Williams 1997a).

Benefit for Few vs. Benefit for Many

Does it matter if a few persons get the most benefit, or should improvement be more equitably distributed throughout the community or plan? Table 19 illustrated that a hypothetical 5 percent increase in HALEs over some period of time for the average community of 250,000 persons

TABLE 20. Two Examples of Equal and Unequal Per Capita Health Improvement

	YHL/person		# persons		YHLs
A.	2.25	×	250,000	=	556,000
B.	10.00	×	10,000	=	100,000
	3.90	×	65,000	=	256,000
	2.25	×	100,000	=	100,000
	0.00	×	50,000	=	0
	− 1.00	×	25,000	=	− 25,000
			250,000		556,000

resulted in 11,658 million HALEs over the baseline of 11,100 million, a growth of 556,000 HALEs. On average, each person began with 44.4 expected future years of healthy life (11,100 million/250,000) and gained 2.25 HALEs (556,000/250,000) from the 5 percent improvement.

The formula for total population HALEs improvement is therefore: POP HALE = individual HALE increase × # persons increasing. This means that the same increase in population HALEs could come from different numbers of persons getting different levels of increase, as shown in table 20.

In both cases, the population of 250,000 gains 556,000 HALEs. But in example A, all 250,000 receive an average of 2.25 per person. In example B, different individuals get different amounts, including some with none and some with less.

It has been suggested that QALY "egalitarianism" implies that the society is indifferent to either of the preceding results, or as it is often stated more simply, to one person getting all 10 possible QALYs or 100 persons getting 0.1 each. This is known as the "aggregation" issue in ethics. Many articles have been written on this (Nord 1994), and Olsen has put this into a quantitative framework, arguing that some equity is called for in giving "some to many rather than many to a few," and suggesting that a "social adjustment factor" be added into the incentives for this purpose (Olsen 1994).

A Purchasing Population Health framework would require that data on past or proposed distribution of improvement across the population be clearly identified so that purchasers and patients can make judgments on whether the distribution of benefits is fair according to their standard of equity.

Is Everyone's Health Equal in Value?

Should other social values (such as having dependents) be given higher priority in determining population health improvement? This concern has several difficult components. The first is whether a greater weight or value for health status increases should be given to groups of individuals for some social purpose, above and beyond the "need" or "capacity to benefit" discussed previously. One example might be elderly or disabled persons, just discussed in this chapter. Another suggestion has been that those who care for dependents be given higher priority by society; therefore, given two individuals of the same age and health status, the value of a hip replacement or treatment for depression would be less for a person living alone than for someone caring for children or elder parents. Williams has carried out beginning survey work in this area, with initial results showing that the public in Britain is equally divided; the most prominent finding has been that of respondents conferring greater weight to those who were "caring for children" (Williams 1988). With regard to the Oregon Health Plan discussed in chapter 6, it is possible that such considerations were implicitly used by the citizen panels as they made adjustments to the "technical" list. In addition, different purchasers or communities may place different values on the trade-offs in HALE improvement resulting from increased quantity or quality of life and/or number of persons benefiting. In my view, this aspect is enormously difficult and complex from an ethical/value perspective and does not need to be resolved until future stages of outcome purchasing.

Distribution of Health Facilities and Providers

Is the level of utilization or access to services a relevant ethical (distributional) consideration? Considerable previous work has focused on lack of equity in health resource allocation, such as the variation in expenditures, hospitals, and physicians across different populations. This focus has been in part due to the fact that such data is more readily available, as well as to the simple assumption shown in figure 2 that the provision of health care reduces disease. Health resources are certainly one factor in the health production function, but they are process measures not fully linked to health outcomes. Resource availability needs to be considered as well as geographic and cultural accessibility, but simple equity in health utilization or access is not an adequate measure of equity in distribution of population health.

However, having a large number of persons without insurance or facing geographic and cultural barriers to access means that they may not be able to derive the benefit from medical care outlined in chapter 5. The United States must find some mix of public and private resources to cover the uninsured as a very high priority as we move to outcomes based purchasing—such a system is of no use to those for whom no purchasing is possible. The movement to cover all children under discussion in Congress and many states in 1997 is a hopeful development that needs support from all concerned about population health improvement.

Is This Social Engineering?

A person reviewing this aspect of Purchasing Population Health might conclude that this is a major program of social engineering. Obviously, reforming the health care system has significant social implications, but the inequities and inefficiencies of the current system have their own set of social implications as well. While there is no technically "correct" answer to any of these ethical or distributional issues, patients, health care purchasers, and the collective public need to consider and resolve these issues since a sense of fairness is a fundamental characteristic of modern democratic society.

The outcome purchasing perspective of this book argues that attention to distribution is necessary, since market forces fail to take such equity considerations fully into account. In fact, existing mechanisms ration implicitly (i.e., produce differential access to benefit), with results that do not yield the most value for the dollars spent and do not consider equity from any perspective other than ability to pay for care. Even the federal Medicare program, which do not discriminate by income, does not have mechanisms for allocating resources for persons or plans with greater capacity to benefit.

Purchasing Population Health argues that such distributional considerations must be made explicit, so that purchasers and consumers can openly judge how resource allocations should be made.

If this is social engineering by some definition, it does not envision or intend the grand and manipulating connotation that this term often implies.

In fact, this is the only way that the ethical issues in HALE distribution could be considered at this stage of the development of such an approach. Health plans (and perhaps later whole communities) should first be required to demonstrate the overall level of HALE improvement (or decline), with appropriate adjustment for different initial levels of health status. In the beginning, financial incentives and rewards would be focused on relative improvement. But each community or plan could be required by the public or private purchaser to provide data on the distributional issues raised previously, and these could be reviewed to determine if adjustments were desirable in the future. The Oregon Plan and the "base closing" analogy discussed in chapter 6 are places to begin. A common standard would not be necessary or even desirable since different communities or purchasers would probably have different values and goals in terms of equity. In all likelihood, however, after a period of time of reviewing performance across multiple communities and plans, a range of generally acceptable distributional norms would begin to emerge.

Summary

This chapter has reviewed the distributional and ethical issues with regard to the fairness of aligning health resources to health outcomes. It concludes that there is no "right" distributional formula or mechanism, either technically or from a values perspective. On the other hand, purchasers and patients have a right to know and have some say in answer to the question, Is simply providing more HALEs appropriate?

The concluding chapters will consider how this could be accomplished in practical terms and the price of not embarking on such a new course. With regard to the issues of equity and fairness discussed here, "you can't manage what you can't measure." This underlies the whole Purchasing Population Health idea but certainly applies to the distributional considerations explored here. It is time to bring implicit or silent decisions into the open and have this evidence available for public and professional debate and resolution.

9 · Making It Happen

The managers of health care resources are stewards of a powerful and magnificent product of human ingenuity. One of our chief responsibilities, despite preoccupation with the survival of our own enterprise, is to constantly push forward the frontiers of service and concern for the society we serve.
—Martin Cherkasky, 1992

We now turn to the possibilities of and challenges to the development of a Purchasing Population Health strategy. Previous chapters have made an argument for the importance of a uniform aggregate measure of health outcome such as HALE as a management tool for purchasing health. This chapter will discuss how such an approach could be realistically incorporated by private and public purchasers of medical care and those responsible for the nonmedical determinants of health sectors and services. It will address the question asked by medical care providers: How will such changes in incentives affect what I do in my clinical practice every day? School, social service, and environmental administrators and practitioners will have similar concerns.

How might it work? The fundamental innovation, truly deserving of the sometimes overused "paradigm shift" phrase, would be aligning financial incentives and rewards for improved outcomes, instead of for individual treatment (fee for service) or packaged (managed care) medical services. This "technical" change would stand much of our current incentive structure on its head, with considerable shifts in provider behavior aimed at improving overall health outcomes.

It is still necessary to discuss the implementation of medical care and nonmedical determinants separately, because of the difficulties in integration across these sectors as discussed in chapter 7. Recall that in Presentville 1997, many medical care providers were still paid on a fee-for-service basis for the individual care they rendered, and managed care plans received an annual amount per person (the capitation rate) up front, in exchange for agreeing to provide all or most medical services needed during the coming year. Investments in nonmedical

I would like to acknowledge the stimulation provided by my students in the Administrative Medicine Graduate Program at the University of Wisconsin and particularly Scott Stringer, M.D., Dennis Uehara, M.D., Margie Bowles, M.D., and Jim Glenski, M.D., whose ideas are referred to in this chapter.

determinants such as in education or the environment were at best weakly tied to their role in improving health outcomes.

In Healthopolis 2020, purchasers will have moved to paying managed care systems for health outcome performance, either on absolute terms or in relationship to other managed care plans on a competitive basis. Initially, a portion of the annual per capita payment could be withheld by the purchaser (employer groups, Medicare, or the states for Medicaid) and awarded retrospectively based on absolute level of improvement in health adjusted life expectancy. Similar financing mechanisms (withholds) are currently used in managed care for other purposes, and retrospective adjustments are also common. As more experience with the system is gained, increasing amounts would be set aside for rewarding improvements in HALE. As Purchasing Population Health matured, linkages to resources and outcome performance of the non–medical care determinants would be incorporated. A fundamental shift would be made from competing on price to competing on outcomes; competitive mechanisms would work in the interest of health outcomes of the members instead of only for plan profits. In some cases, medical care systems may target more investments to the less healthy populations, rather than avoiding these groups, since their potential for health outcome improvement could be greater and more cost effective.

This book is written in the hope that it will stimulate active discussion and debate about Purchasing Population Health. Although this is not an idea that could be fully implemented immediately, it is not unrealistic that much of what is suggested here could be well under way by the second decade of the twenty-first century. This chapter will outline the following three phases of potential development and implementation over the next 15 years:

Phase 1 (1997–2000)	Debate, acceptance, and research
Phase 2 (2001–10)	Outcome based payment for integrated health delivery systems
Phase 3 (2011–20)	Incorporating the nonmedical determinants and sectors

Phase 1 (1997–2000): Debate, Acceptance, and Research

The first four years will be dominated by continued medical care system consolidation, driven in large part by fiscal constraints from private purchasers as well as from federal and state budget deficit reduction efforts. Those areas of the country just beginning to incorporate managed care will be in greater turmoil, as will Medicare and Medicaid providers as managed care reaches increasing proportions of these populations. Under such pressures, it will be hard for many providers and systems to focus their efforts on group health outcomes. However, measures like HEDIS, discussed in chapter 4, will increasingly incorporate an outcomes approach, and mature markets and progressive states will have opportunity for experimentation.

This period provides a good opportunity for discussion and debate about the framework proposed here, with an optimal result being some public-private consensus on the direction and scope of change. At the same time, research and demonstration efforts can continue to build an empirical and experiential base that implementation of this concept requires. Modest private and public resources devoted to applied analytic efforts such as those listed subsequently would pay handsome dividends in the following decades.

Shifting the Focus of Debate to Value

With regard to debate, it is essential that discussion of changes in the health care sector shift from process issues of reorganization and consolidation to the value issues of outcome and cost. The ultimate goal of changes in health care should be cost-effective improvement in health outcomes. Means of achievement such as universal coverage, cost containment, outcomes/quality assessment, and system reorganization should be considered and evaluated in this context. Debate in the media, in corporate boardrooms, in legislative bodies, and in academia should shift to this perspective.

The debate should not be framed in terms of party politics, because both U.S. conservatives and liberals favor getting the maximum return in health outcomes from private and public investments. For liberals, this is viewed as moving toward a more rational and egalitarian distribution of a social good. From a conservative perspective, it is seen as providing more complete information to purchasers on health outcomes so that market forces operate more effectively. Both of these perspectives have merit and are relevant to the current political debate in Congress (Medicare) and in state legislatures (Medicaid) on how to reduce public expenditures for health care without sacrificing quality.

Who Monitors Performance?

An important issue to be considered during this phase is that of data responsibility and accountability. It will have to be decided if such outcome data collection and analysis are a provider, purchaser (employer coalition, Medicare), or public (health department, state insurance commissioner) responsibility (Gosfield 1997; Riley 1997; Lee and Paxman 1997). In the discussion of reinventing public health associated with the 1994 Health Security Act, the locus of such outcome data and assessment was proposed as a possible public health responsibility, although these suggestions did not go so far as to consider data from all determinants of health.

The goal of discussion and debate for phase 1 is to reach some level of public acceptance of this new Purchasing Population Health paradigm, in which financial incentives will be tied to demonstrated outcomes instead of to inputs or processes as is currently the accepted practice. After this, implementation in two phases will insure that these incentives are incorporated into fundamental financial and managerial mechanisms so that optimal value in terms of health outcomes can be achieved.

Phase 2 (2001–10): Outcome Based Payment for Integrated Health Delivery Systems

In the second phase it should be possible to see outcome based payment for fully integrated (seamless) medical care systems, which go beyond hospital and physician integration to include prevention, primary care, long-term care, and health education. Financial mechanisms should begin to reward systems for the aspects of HALE improvement under their control. What kind of specific incentives would work?

Someone having read this far will understand the pitfalls of adopting process measures (such as a mammography screening rate) for outcome performance, because they do not indicate the ultimate outcome (how many women develop or die from breast cancer). On the other hand, producing better outcomes can only be done through changes in the structure and processes in medical care and the other determinants of health. Berwick has identified the following 11 "worthy aims" for clinical leadership for "better outcomes, greater ease of use, lower cost, and more social justice in health status" (Berwick 1994):

1. Reduce inappropriate surgery, admissions, and tests
2. Reduce underlying root causes of illness such as smoking and injury
3. Reduce Cesarean section rates below 10 percent
4. Reduce unwanted and ineffective end of life procedures
5. Adopt simplified formularies and streamline pharmaceuticals
6. Increase patient participation in decision making
7. Decrease delays and waiting of all types
8. Reduce inventory levels
9. Record only useful information and only once
10. Reduce the total supply of high technology medical and surgical care and consolidate it into regional centers
11. Reduce the racial gap in health status beginning with infant mortality and low birth weight

Berwick's list is a good example of important strategies for any system wanting to affect health outcomes. It is a combination of structure, process, and outcome actions. Although the relative improvement per dollar invested in each is not specified, the ideas on his list are the type that clinicians and their organizations can and are beginning to implement now. When financial incentives for outcomes are in place, such actions will become the rule rather than the exception.

Such initial steps in the medical care domain are within our reach and should be routinely implemented in this phase. This is a period that holds great promise for demonstration projects to begin testing aspects of purchasing for outcomes prior to full implementation. Many of these are under way already, including some of the Healthy Communities projects of the HealthCare Forum, the Kellogg Community Care Demonstrations, and a number of local initiatives, often in the public health and prevention domain. The list in table 21 identifies only a few of the Healthy Community activities currently being carried out in communities all across the nation (*Healthcare Forum Journal* 1997).

As important as such projects are, however, history tells us that they are not enough. Some are developed primarily for marketing and public relations purposes, while others are supported on marginal revenue streams and depend on the goodwill of a particular manager or foundation. Health outcomes are too important to be left to even well meaning efforts on the margin of the health care system.

TABLE 21.   1996 Healthier Communities Awards

Westwood, Colorado—vacant building purchase and renovation; volunteer training for home bound elderly; youth conflict resolution training

River Falls, Wisconsin—after school youth recreational, educational, and employment opportunities; adolescent alcohol prevention, community resource center

South Bend, Indiana—health and quality-of-life issue identification; six community wide councils; regional center for children with special needs

Springfield, Massachusetts—immunization registry, youth career counseling and employment assistance, guarantee of at least one health professional in every school

Tallinn, Estonia—Estonian Centre for Health Education and Promotion sponsored 16 nationwide health promotion workshops to develop priorities and implementation strategies.

Source: Healthcare Forum Journal 1997.

Early Beginnings

Some communities and organizations are beginning to experiment with integrating such activities into financial mechanisms and incentives, in response to challenges from health plans to show them that purchasers are serious about outcomes. One health plan set aside budgeted incentive payments that demonstrated improvement in primary care, specialty care, and experimental therapy outcomes. Outcomes rewarded included immunization rates, time to return to work after knee surgery, and coverage of experimental therapies not regularly covered but with promising outcome indications (Isham 1997). Many other purchasers are building "performance purchasing" into managed care contract requirements, with financial penalties for nonperformance on certain outcomes measures. Some national plans have begun to provide financial incentives for employees who choose providers who rank more highly on quality measures.

Going beyond acute care, Medicare Social HMO demonstrations are integrating payment for different components of health care, and the State of Wisconsin has announced plans to integrate payments across medical care, nursing home, and home care services for elderly and disabled persons (*Wisconsin State Journal* 1997). Such programs could be the first to experiment with outcome based payment for such vertically integrated systems.

In my class in population health for midcareer physician executives, I ask students to write a final paper discussing what different programs and health determinants they would invest in if 10 percent of their system's capitation was withheld by the regional purchasing coalition or Medicare and placed in a competitive pool for return to the systems that showed the most improvement in the health status of their populations. Given the size of most of their health plans, the amount at risk would be $4 to $8 million. Listen to the clinical and preventive interventions these experienced clinician managers identified for additional investment to improve health outcomes:

- smoking cessation
- prenatal care
- chronic disease management
- adolescent and elderly trauma
- asthma prevention and treatment
- complete immunizations program
- cancer screening
- increased treatment of depression

Note that these are not only prevention programs. They also represent additional investments above the amounts already being spent for such programs under existing incentives.

In an even more concrete assessment of potential interventions, two students suggested specific investment strategies, which are shown in the following. In the first, the plan includes 30,000 Medicaid enrollees and 50,000 commercial enrollees. The 10 percent health status withhold amounted to $12,000,000, and the executive decided to invest half of it, or $6,000,000, in the following programs to improve health outcomes:

Smoking cessation	$960,000
Prenatal care coordination	$1,900,000
Depression screening and treatment	$960,000
Asthmatic patient education	$960,000
School based clinics	$573,000
County nurse outreach	$1,000,000

The second suggestion was for a Medicaid plan of 87,000 children. The withhold was $5.3 million, and this executive decided to invest all of it in the following way:

Education and health promotion	$450,000
Screening and immunization	$120,000
School based clinics	$4,500,000
Infant mortality reduction	$500,000
Head Start enhancement	$170,000

These are, of course, only hypothetical examples, and both of them focus mainly on mothers and children, reflecting the nature of the population; a strategy for an exclusively Medicare population would have a different emphasis. But they illustrate how actual health plan managers might make different or enhanced investments under a Purchasing Population Health financial incentive system.

How Will New Incentives Change Behavior?

Providers often ask,

How will this change what I do every day in the hospital or clinic?

This is a critically important question, both for understanding and acceptance and for effective implementation. Figure 44 is a representation of these relationships in phase 2. Financial incentives are applied at the health plan–integrated system level, so that the managers at that level will be motivated to support and ensure changes that improve health outcomes throughout the system. They will work actively with the delivery settings in their system such as hospitals, physician practices, nursing homes, and home health providers in a variety of ways.

First, there will be some clinical activities that will either be required or prohibited by administrative rule. Examples of required activities would be (1) providing only generic drugs when they are as effective as the more expensive brand names and (2) mandating an immunization or cancer screening policy for all patients of a certain age. Second, a set of incentives would be issued in a series of outcome guidelines; these would be encouraged but would have flexibility in local implementation. Examples would be guidelines for Cesarean sec-

FIG. 44. HALE financial incentives and delivery systems.

tion or under age 50 mammography screening. Third, resources for new program development would be made available, perhaps based on a competition among new ideas submitted from the delivery settings or individual providers. These would be for ideas that show promise for improving outcomes but that first need to be tested. Financial rewards would be aligned with outcome improvement in individual delivery settings, so that those institutions, plans, or providers who make the most contribution to population outcome improvements would be rewarded. Since overall population health improvement is being measured, it is not likely that the work of any individual physician, nurse, or social worker would be rewarded personally, but certainly group efforts could be rewarded in some equitable manner such as end of year bonuses.

Interventions and programs like these are currently being implemented in many health plans but they are primarily focused on cost reductions—adding a health outcome component would shift attention away from only cost considerations to a primary emphasis on value in terms of results per unit of resources expended.

Financial Incentive Mechanisms

The tasks of being sure the financial reward mechanisms are designed appropriately must be taken very seriously, since some portion of one-seventh of the nation's economy will be affected by them. Managed care plans are currently paid on an average monthly per capita basis, with most of these resources utilized to maintain current levels of health care services; health status improvement is implicitly desired but not adequately measured or explicitly rewarded. A decision would have to be made as to whether improvement incentive payments should be included within baseline amounts or as additional incentives. Providers might argue that improvements will not be possible if the baseline is reduced, and therefore incentive payments should be additional. But there is wide variation in current per capita expenditures across the states, only partially explained by price and other demographic factors (Kindig and Libby 1994), so caution should be used in adopting current levels as "baseline" in all regions of the country.

If health status improvement were the only goal, then private or public purchasers could develop a health status improvement fund that would be awarded retrospectively to different providers in relation to their outcomes. If cost containment is also a goal, a basic capitation rate could be developed adjusted for baseline HALE, with a certain amount withheld for retrospective awards.

Developing such a rate has many of the issues associated with traditional risk adjustment, except that the variation of concern is initial level of health status (capacity to benefit adjusted) rather than utilization or expenditures, as was described in chapter 8.

Rewarding for Long-Term Improvements

In chapter 5 the issues of time and latency were introduced, with the example of the three British towns (table 13). It is essential for a health outcome financing strategy to reward both for improvement in the short run and for long-term outcomes. This is particularly critical given the short (monthly) enrollment periods in some managed care programs. Mortality changes occur in the long run, but if plans and communities have the degree of variation seen in table 2 (chap. 2), initially greater incentives in the short run could be given to those with more capacity to benefit (i.e., areas with higher mortality rates), assuming that investments were targeted to efforts (reviewed and approved by the private or public payer) that reflected an agreed upon improvement strategy. Also in the short run, more immediate rewards could be targeted to improvement in the disability or morbidity components of the HALE index; to the degree that such measures are manipulable, safeguards will need to be in place. Longer term retrospective rewards for HALE improvement would also have to be developed, to provide incentive for 5 to 10 year progress as well. As discussed in chapter 8, public information and open mechanisms for reviewing the distribution of improvement between payers and providers will be required.

Preventing Manipulation

Whoever has the data collecting and monitoring responsibility discussed earlier will need to develop ongoing efforts to detect intentional gaming or unintended consequences of the new incentives (Luft 1996). Significant attention needs to be devoted to tracking changes in the denominator as persons move across plans and communities. Some may view such movement as a fundamental problem with an outcomes purchasing approach, but this should be less problematic as managed care markets mature and stabilize and everyone has access to health insurance. There is no doubt that new and creative quantitative approaches for incorporating such changes in population denominators will have to be developed.

Smith indicates a series of "unintended consequences" of managing to performance indicators (such as tunnel vision, suboptimization, and gaming) and suggests strategies for dealing with them (Smith 1995). Finally, an assessment must be made of the costs of data collection and health status improvement measurement to be sure that cost-effectiveness considerations apply here as well.

Phase 3 (2011–20): Incorporating the Nonmedical Determinants and Sectors

Phase 2 would be a remarkable achievement in itself. Why not stop there and celebrate our success? The temptation is present, but the job would not be done, since, as we saw in chapter 5, health outcomes are achieved not only by medical care but also by other determinants of health such as socioeconomic status and the environment operating independently. In terms of additional health outcome improvement in the United States, these factors may be more important than medical advances, as impressive as these will be.

But how can the determinants not under the control of medical systems, even broadly defined, be integrated with the medical care sector? Chapter 7 outlined current theory and practice to meet this challenge. An initial step, which could happen either immediately or in phase 2, might be that powerful integrated delivery systems could exert corporate social responsibility by investing directly in, or influencing, local expenditures in related sectors such as education, social services, and the environment. Listen to the proposals made by physician executives for nonclinical investments to further improve the health of their populations and to increase their chances to win back the health outcome lottery withhold:

- lobbying for health education programs in schools
- influencing welfare reform at the state level
- redirecting employee educational tuition resources to reading improvement for children and adults
- dedicating a percentage of health system employment opportunities for low-income individuals
- establishing a Department of Community and Social Health that would ensure that all plan members have strong social and community connections
- establishing a government relations service to support healthy public policy at the local and state levels
- paying for public day care

Another comprehensive approach proposed the allocation of the $30 million withhold from a population of 250,000 in the following way:

- $24 million to improve socioeconomic status through minimum wage subsidy, job search and training, housing coordination, and child care and preschool programs
- $2 million in "social capital" investments such as youth athletics, voter registration, and civic organization grants
- $700,000 in healthy lifestyle programs such as health/lifestyle screening and smoking cessation/prevention
- $300,000 in prenatal care and teen mothers support
- $800,000 in youth investment such as sex education, sexually transmitted disease (STD) prevention, accident prevention, and teen violence prevention
- $2,000,000 in long-term care coordination

Coordinating Health Outcomes across Sectors

Going beyond such efforts originating in health plans or delivery systems are demonstrations to bring medical care and social services closer together, mentioned in chapter 7. These have been proposed and/or are being implemented in England with joint commissioning between medical care and social services; in some Canadian provinces such as Prince Edward Island, where all resources for health, education, and social services are being administered from a common fund and structure; and in Sweden, where a public health committee of cabinet ministers to

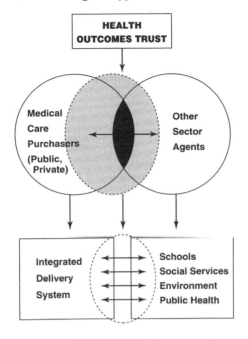

FIG. 45. Integrating the determinants of health.

integrate policy across health, education, labor, and housing has recently been developed. Figure 45 indicates how this might be concep-
tualized in phase 3.

For simplicity, two governing agents are shown, one being the
private and public purchaser of medical care and a second for the primarily public nonmedical determinant sectors (realizing that each component of the second, like education and the environment, is a sector in
its own right). At the current time there is little intersection between
these two components, as represented by the smaller black area of the
overlapping circles. As we move through phase 3, this intersection ex-
pands in the direction of the arrows, creating the larger gray overlapping
space within the dotted lines. This new, expanded intersection penetrates medical care purchasers more fully, as a result of the fact that
health outcomes are the only responsibility of these purchasing agents.
In contrast, while the nonmedical sectors have a component of their
activity that produces health outcomes, another component is devoted
to other purposes beyond health outcomes (such as education for employment, environment for beauty). For this reason the dotted intersection penetrates this circle less fully.

The intersecting space is labeled the Health Outcomes Trust, indicating that some set of agents or relationships will have to take responsibility for creating intersectoral incentives for health outcome improvement. The Trust will have responsibility for stimulating a new set of collaborative initiatives, indicated by the dotted lines and arrows between the integrated health care delivery systems and the schools, social service agencies, and environmental programs. Examples of these could include the previously mentioned health programs in schools, joint efforts at violence prevention, neighborhood improvement efforts, and employee safety and absenteeism reduction programs. These relationships are similar to those suggested by Shortell in his vision of a Community Health Management System (Shortell et al. 1996).

Since such coordination has not yet been effectively demonstrated, it has been placed in a time period approximately 15 years from now because workable methods need to be developed. But lest it seem totally fanciful, listen to the vision of another physician executive:

> The creation of such a community group is to catalyze vision and community problem solving for improving health. Such a group will inevitably result in the advancement of political agendas by individual and subgroup stakeholders. However, if it can pass through this stage of self-interest, it can develop an agenda for population health.
>
> When one thinks of the determinants of health, they are divided into medical and nonmedical components. The medical determinants are what physicians classically think of as health and are within the domain of medicine. The nonmedical determinants are varied and are usually the responsibility of public and private organizations such as schools, public health, social services, and employers. Managing boundaries and integrating the various systems is one way to collaborate in population health improvement. But is it the only way?
>
> An alternative view is that if borders are intrusive, either blur them or get rid of them. If health improvement is best delivered by several community agencies, can a new entity be developed which is made up, in part or in whole, by these several agencies? Will the CEO of the future population health delivery system preside over an integrated health care system/public health/education/social service/employer coalition? One can envision

the leader of such a system allocating scarce resources to the determinants of health that will best improve the health of the community. As the leader of an "integrated population health delivery system," there should be no bias for a particular determinant. The resources for all the determinants of health will be in one budget and responsibility for health improvement assigned to one agency.

This scenario is not one likely to occur in the near term. However, as the significance of the nonmedical determinants of health becomes more appreciated, and the cost of medical care continues to rise, the importance of integration of all agencies responsible for improvement becomes critical.

This is one compelling and articulate view. But a seamless and efficient integration of the largely private medical care systems and the largely public other determinants in the United States will await forms of integration across these sectors not yet developed in theory or practice. In Europe and Canada it is easier to imagine governmental leadership for such coordination, since often health care and the other sectors are under public control. In the United States this poses unique challenges, since medical care is primarily delivered in the private sector, while most of the other determinants are in the public sectors. Lessons from other countries need to be explored for relevance, but undoubtedly new models will be required here. In all likelihood such models will involve "virtual" rather than "ownership" integration strategies, with networking and collaborative relationships to insure appropriate boundaries and resource allocation (Goldsmith 1994). The lessons from the environmental sector mentioned in chapter 7 need considerably more careful examination for relevance. The development of such integration models and assessment of sectoral responsibility will be a high priority for the initial decade of the twenty-first century.

First Steps: Medicare, Medicaid, and the States

One excellent place to begin to work toward realistic implementation of such a strategy is with the Medicare population. There are several reasons for this. The first is that this is a large program, and the fact that it is under federal "single payer" auspices means that consistent standards can be developed more easily across geographic subpopulations. Much of the Medicare program is moving to capitated managed care contracts, with more than 10 percent of patients now under such a system. The rapid expansion of Medicare managed care has raised concerns from politicians and patients regarding both quality and outcomes. In addition, as previously mentioned, the Medicare SHMO program has been one of the few in the United States to integrate acute care and some aspects of long-term care. Medicare has already been experimenting with innovative approaches to outcome measurement in its Medicare Beneficiary Health Status Registry and in its plans for Beneficiary-Centered Purchasing; these efforts, cited in chapter 3, should be rapidly expanded. Finally, there is a good track record of Medicare innovations spreading to the private health insurance and purchaser sector. It is also possible for Medicaid to take a role in the development of Purchasing Population Health, because more than one-third of its recipients already are enrolled in managed care plans. Medicaid has the disadvantage of being 50 separate state programs, but this could be an advantage in allowing for different experimental models with a central evaluation component.

But Medicare cannot easily coordinate the inputs from the other health determinant sectors. It is possible and might be advantageous to develop some mechanism for national coordination and guidance (such as the Swedish Cabinet Minister's Council or Ilona Kickbush's "Departments of Consequences" mentioned in chapter 7 [Kickbush 1994]), but in the United States much of this activity (such as education, welfare, public health, environmental regulation) is under state and local rather than federal control. The possibility exists for several cutting edge states (Oregon's Benchmarks project comes most readily to mind) where perhaps a megaintegrated activity across all health enhancing sectors, including local, state, and federal agents under block grant authority, could be designed and carried out for a five year demonstration period, even in phase 2. This would have similarities to the activity under way in Prince Edward Island and could benefit from their early experiences. Such a limited demonstration would not be too expensive to carry out in a few carefully designed settings; perhaps this could be tried soon under federal, state, and private sector funding and oversight. Results from these experiments might then be available for broader implementation in phases 2 and 3 when federal deficit reduction has been accomplished, when the medical system has matured in its consolidation, and when pressures for more cost-effective health outcomes are even higher.

Research Tasks

There are a number of research and demonstration tasks that deserve urgent attention, such as those listed below. In some cases, resolving the research questions will be essential for the debate and discussion to be adequately concluded.

Research Task No. 1. Refinement and acceptance of standard measures of population health outcome. This is the most important initial challenge for research and development, since without an agreed upon measure of outcome as discussed in chapter 4 (with safeguards to prevent manipulation) payment cannot be linked to it: "you can't manage what you can't measure." Assuming acceptance of some aggregate health adjusted life expectancy framework, there is considerable work required to refine one or a set of measures such as outlined in chapter 4. Attention must be paid to both mortality and morbidity/quality components of any HALE measure. Regarding mortality, since death records are in the public domain, mechanisms need to be developed for managed care plans to be able to track the mortality of members of their plans, or in their geographic locations, particularly if private managed care systems are the primary agents for at least the medical determinants of health. The possibility of using life expectancy at different ages (infants, children, young adults, middle aged, and aged) for the HALE mortality component also needs consideration, since this may indicate which type of investment will be most effective in different populations.

For the morbidity/disability/quality component of HALE, it is necessary to find measures to reliably assess both baseline and future improvement (Fryback et al. 1993). Roos and Shapiro have recently published the impressive experience and early results from the Population Based Health Information System in Manitoba (Roos and Shapiro 1995; Roos et al. 1996). They indicate that outcome indicators must have the following characteristics: scientific credibility, administrative availability, clear definitions, and high enough numbers to produce valid statistics. McHorney has recently observed that there is a tension between the "fidelity" (accuracy) of a generic measure and its "bandwidth" (how much it covers) (McHorney 1996). This is a challenge for the measurement framework proposed here, since it has emphasized the need for simple broad measures to compare both the baseline and subsequent change for large groups of health plans or community members. The cost of collecting these data must also be carefully assessed, for it would compromise the entire Purchasing Population Health effort to require very expensive data collection and analysis.

Research Task No. 2. The "need" for health in various populations: moving beyond risk adjustment. This is of critical importance, since, as was seen in chapter 8, it is likely that different populations will have different initial levels of health status and therefore will require different types and amounts of intervention and investment. Assuming that "need" for health maintenance or improvement is defined as the Williams concept of "capacity to benefit" (Williams 1974), the analytic job of determining such capacity is substantial. Research into the Fielding concept of "ameliorability" (Fielding 1995) would be central here, so that an assessment could be made regarding the potential for differential investment strategies; recall the discussion in chapter 8 regarding populations with higher levels of genetic disease, environmental factors, or AIDS or lower socioeconomic status. This is why it was suggested earlier that HALE measures for different age groups might be useful, since it is likely that improvement or ameliorability from medical care or other determinants will vary across age groups (i.e., reduction of infant mortality vs. chronic illness in the elderly).

This is closely related to the current efforts in health risk adjustment (Iezzoni 1994), but most work in the risk adjustment field is done from an actuarial insurance perspective. Giacomini and colleagues state that there are two policy goals of risk adjustment: (1) to allow consumers to compare premium differences that are not distorted by health risk differences between the plan's members but rather vary with the plan's value and efficiency; and (2) to reimburse each plan fairly for the population health risk that the plan assumes (Giacomini, Luft, and Robinson 1995). In practice, most attention is devoted to variations in expenditure, not outcomes, since this is what the plans must manage and minimize in the current incentive structure. Very little variation in expenditure is explained by traditional variables of age and gender; this should not be surprising, given the large impact that variation in price, utilization, and the supply of doctors and hospitals have on total expenditures. The work in risk adjustment needs to shift to focus on the different needs that populations have for health outcome improvement, instead of simply on expenditure levels (Fowles et al. 1996). Once the outcome goal is defined correctly, more appropriate investment will follow as providers are rewarded for the most efficient improvement in health outcomes.

The set of analytic issues concerning time and latency also needs attention in this phase, in order to develop incentives for a balanced short-run and long-run approach. As discussed in chapter 5, different factors in population health status have an impact over different time periods; that is, an epidemic or a new immunization or a new form of hip replacement might have immediate impact while education is presumably gained primarily in childhood with impact over a lifetime.

Research Task No. 3. Cross-sectoral cost-effectiveness research. In order to move to integrating the nonmedical determinants of health, a Purchasing Population Health strategy will need the support of extensive additional cost-effectiveness research on all of the non–health care determinants of health. For all the criticism that medical care receives, studies of cost-effectiveness of various medical interventions and programs are much more advanced than in other health determinants. The debate over national standards for educational outcomes has similarities to the need for health outcomes. Drummond and colleagues have recently called for such a cross-sectoral framework for health status cost-effectiveness analysis, but almost no work exists in this field at this time (Drummond and Stoddart 1995; Drummond, Torrance, and Mason 1993). Exceptions to this lack of studies were identified in chapter 6: the work of Drummond and colleagues themselves, who identified the cost of improvement in quality of life for the caregivers of demented elderly persons, and the research of Tengs and colleagues, who have examined the evidence for 500 lifesaving interventions crossing several sectors from a risk analytic perspective (Tengs et al. 1995) (see table 15). Since such research is not supported by many traditional sources, new financing mechanisms must be established to be sure such critical work is accomplished in the future.

Research Task No. 4. Other distributional issues including social valuation of HALEs. The remaining ethical and distributional issues identified in chapter 8 also need to be addressed. These include ensuring that subpopulations such as the elderly and the disabled are not discriminated against in an outcomes framework. This concern has to be paired with the related concept of social valuation, such as exemplified in the initial work of Williams, in which he found that some British citizens believed that certain individuals such as those "caring for children" should have their HALE maintenance or improvement weighted higher (Williams 1988). This would by definition discriminate against other groups, but presumably with a higher order of social consensus. The process of ranking medical interventions in Oregon needs to be reviewed for guidance as to how to approach such choices in a broader framework. Of course, the Oregon process did not include nonmedical interventions, which would ultimately have to be taken into account in a complete Purchasing Population Health framework.

Research Task No. 5. Population health research support. The complexity of these studies cannot be the entire explanation for lack of progress in this area. It is possible to return to Evans and Stoddart's first thermostatic model of health care and disease (fig. 2) and assert that society's general acceptance of this simple explanation has also determined the lack of research investment focused on the nonmedical determinants of health. Federal 1996 biomedical research expenditures were $11.9 billion, compared to $125 million in studies of the kind suggested here. One does not have to be an enemy of biological and clinical science to wonder about these relative priorities given the evidence that multiple factors are responsible for health status. Increased public and private research support for the questions identified here will be essential; as indicated earlier, much of this will come from delivery organizations themselves as they search for answers when operating under revised financial incentives.

Summary

This chapter has demonstrated that Purchasing Population Health is not just a theoretical concept but one that can be developed and implemented over the next several decades. It envisions revising the fundamental economic incentives that have been applied to one-seventh of our economy for half a century. Using HALE as a health outcome purchasing standard would encourage a gradual and almost invisible transition in the direction of cost-effective health outcome improvement.

Even so, it is an ambitious undertaking. But are lesser options viable? The final chapter will briefly outline the rationale for taking action and will assess the price of maintaining the status quo.

10 · The Case for Action, the Price of Inertia

"Cheshire Puss," she began, . . . "Would you tell me, please,
which way I ought to go from here?"
"That depends a good deal on where you want to get to," said
the cat.
"I don't much care where . . ." said Alice.
"Then it doesn't matter which way you go," said the cat.
  —Lewis Carroll, *Alice in Wonderland*

This book presents an argument for a fundamental reorientation in measuring and financing health outcomes. We have seen that health expenditures in the United States are by far the highest in the world and are not accompanied by similarly high outcomes. Measuring health outcomes as health adjusted life expectancy (HALE) at the large population level has been proposed as the financial incentive standard for Purchasing Population Health. The existence of multiple determinants of health requires the development of an integrating mechanism across these determinants and the agents responsible for them. A framework for considering distributional issues within populations or health plans has been outlined. Finally, a concrete and realistic plan for debate, research, development, and implementation over the next two decades has been presented.

It might appear in the contemporary United States that purchasers are interested only in price reductions and not in outcomes, and that these ideas are more relevant to other countries which have different values or are under less economic pressure. The challenge of this argument is that a cost perspective is too narrow by itself and will be self-defeating as we move into the final value oriented phase of health system reform. Americans are unusually results oriented, and the organization of large enrolled populations provides potential advantages not enjoyed in other nations still primarily operating on an individual patient basis.

This final chapter addresses the important question of why we should proceed down this different and ambitious path. It includes consideration of why change is needed, why resource constraints make it more urgent, who will benefit, how this concept is consistent with U.S. values and approaches to change, and what the price of the "do nothing" option is.

Why Change?

"If it ain't broke, don't fix it." *"Primum non nocere."* The first is a commonsense phrase; the second is the Latin quotation, "first do no harm," that hung over the delivery room where I did my obstetrics training at the University of Chicago School of Medicine. Why is a Purchasing Population Health reorientation necessary? Can't we get along the way we are, making only marginal changes? Why focus on health care?

This proposal is at the same time simple and profound. Common sense tells us that we should pay for the best result we can get, as we would when we purchase a car, a home, or a bag of potato chips. The complex nature of health outcomes and expenditures, however, renders traditional market forces impotent, since the "perfect information" requirement is difficult to achieve; witness the recent controversy over the advisability of screening mammograms in women from age 40 to 50.

The evidence presented in the first chapter is a compelling rationale: we are spending much more per capita on health care than any other nation in the world; our outcomes are not consistent with these expenditures; and both health expenditures and outcomes have significant variation across the states. Figure 11 deserves review at this point: the difference between the United States $3,331 per capita expenditure and the $1,971 in Canada, $1,835 in Germany, $1,495 in Japan, and $1,213 in the United Kingdom, with little evidence of outcome differences, speaks convincingly for itself. In addition, the 36 percent variation in age adjusted mortality across regions of the United States shown in table 2 cries out for review of the resources allocated to these geographic areas.

On the other hand, reorienting financial incentives for one-seventh of the U.S. economy (and more as nonmedical factors are included) is not to be taken lightly, since the potential for "doing harm" is certainly present. Many employees and industries are doing very well in the current system, and reductions or reorientation of expenditures will produce significant adjustments.

The Limits of a Resource Constrained Environment

Why not therefore view health care expenditure growth, regardless of outcomes, as an economic miracle, one that should be celebrated and enhanced rather than restrained? The answer lies in the fact that much

of health care is financed by employers and government, both functioning in an environment with resource constraints. If resource constraints
were not at issue, then operating on the "flat of the health production
function curve" (fig. 38) would pose no problem, unless interventions
that decreased outcomes were involved. But a United States or a world
with no resource constraints seems highly unlikely in the foreseeable
future or ever. If we truly are not getting value for our health care dollars,
then we could either get increased outcomes for the same expenditure
or similar outcomes for less. If the United States purchased health care
at the rate in Germany, for example, the $1,496 per capita savings would
amount to about $300 billion annually, about 5.6 percent of our econ-
omy. If U.S. health expenditures mirrored the rate of growth of the rest
of the economy, we would have another $750 billion available each year
by 2005. Think of how much could be done with these resources; to
begin with, we could provide health insurance for all the uninsured for
about 10 percent of this amount; we could cover all uninsured children
for about 1 percent.

Who Will Benefit?

The primary beneficiaries of reduced health expenditures, or better outcomes from existing expenditures, will be both individuals and public
and private payers. Individuals will experience longer and better lives;
payers will invest the savings for other private or public purposes.
Within health care, the pressure to provide services to the growing elderly population and to cover the uninsured (which in my mind has to
be a very high priority after federal deficit reduction) will continue to
stress budgets for Medicare, Medicaid, and other public sources of
funds. The number of persons without insurance is rising, and the number of retirees with health benefits is falling, as demonstrated in figures
46 and 47.

The case for serious consideration of a Purchasing Population
Health strategy is also based on the potential for resource reallocation to
health investments of greater value and the need for resources elsewhere in our economy. Going beyond medical care issues, it is apparent
to most that our society has significant needs for resources in areas such
as education, urban development, public safety, drug control, the environment, and public and corporate infrastructure.

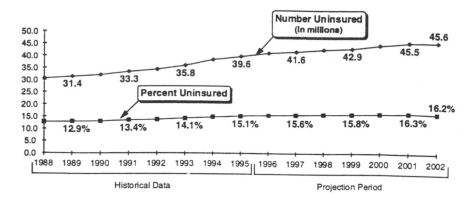

FIG. 46. Growth in uninsured in the United States.
(Lewin Group 1996.)

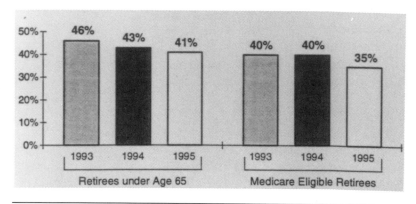

FIG. 47. Percentage of employers offering retiree health coverage.
(Lewin Group 1996.)

The "American Way"

Such potential advantages or imperatives have not been adequate to stimulate cost control or outcome based health care purchasing in the past. Voluntary efforts have not been successful, and regulatory approaches to cost containment, such as those in the Carter administration and embodied in the Clinton Health Security Act, have been roundly rejected (Broder and Johnson 1996). This was never seen more clearly than in the latter debate, which turned quickly to universal coverage and system reorganization, while the important cost-containment proposal, blending market forces and regulatory intervention, was lost. Similarly, it seems likely that significant reductions in Medicare growth rates will be enacted soon in order to reduce the federal deficit and save the Medicare Trust Fund but without any strong linkage to the consequences of these reductions in terms of health outcomes.

It is part of our U.S. revolutionary origins that we are skeptical of government and public intrusion into our private lives and economic decisions. Significant public policy changes occur very rarely and under unusual social and political circumstances, such as Roosevelt's New Deal and the passage of Medicare and Medicaid in the 1960s. The rejection of Medicare catastrophic coverage in 1989 and the Health Security Act in 1994 is more consistent than inconsistent with U.S. views and opinion. Such attitudes are likely to continue, given the historically low public trust in government reflected in public opinion polls.

Despite our reluctance to enact broad public policy changes, we accept readily and are world leaders in technical innovation. Recent examples of this in health care are the development and rapid adoption of Diagnostic Related Groups for Medicare payment, health maintenance organizations, and continuous quality improvement strategies. The approach taken in the Oregon Health Plan discussed in chapter 6 is one example, whatever its limitations, of our ability to approach innovation and change through such mechanisms.

> **Through a mechanism that is more technical in nature, and therefore more consistent with U.S. values and approaches, Purchasing Population Health has significant potential for stimulating improvement in health outcomes per dollar invested. It does not require sweeping national legislation or broad social experimentation but is more analogous to the acceptance of a new purchasing standard such as miles per gallon on a new car or the speed of a computer chip.**

In a simple but profound way, it says that we will define the unit of health outcome at the population or health plan level as health adjusted life expectancy, and that private and public purchasers will pay providers and health plans (and eventually agents of the other determinants) for performance according to such outcome measures. There will be some gradual changes in resource distribution, and some of the answers to the distributional questions posed in chapter 8 will be controversial. But a Purchasing Population Health framework will put these considerations in a considerably more objective framework, as opposed to one that is primarily invisible or subjective and political.

A Climate of Creativity and Innovation

Purchasing Population Health will stimulate creativity and innovation such as health care delivery has never seen. As opposed to only public health demonstrations, public and private sector agents operating under this new financial incentive structure will devise thousands of innovations and cost benefit assessments impossible to imagine today. The beneficiaries of this innovation will cross all sectors of the United States . . . businesses, government, and, of course, individual patients.

The Price of Inertia

It is possible that some other approach would be equally effective in getting more value for our health care investments, but none has been proposed or is under development. Marginal solutions have failed, in part because of the complexity of the product and in part because of the power of vested professional and corporate interests in maintaining the status quo. Major demonstrations such as the Office of Economic Opportunity South Bronx Neighborhood Health Center were not flawed in concept but failed because they were funded by grants that ran their course and were not incorporated into ongoing financial or managerial processes.

The "do nothing" option is occasionally appropriate, but in the case of U.S. health care in 1997 it will at best result in marginal changes in outcomes at similar levels of investment. At the worst, the price of inertia or doing nothing denies the opportunity for greater levels of health at current levels of expenditure and/or for reduced medical expenditure and reallocation of resources to other determinants of health.

From Presentville 1997 to Healthopolis 2020

The challenge of this book is to make the basic shift in financial incentives and outcomes performance that Healthopolis 2020 envisions. Our public and private resources are too precious not to be used for optimal value for health or any other social purpose. The fundamental assertion of this book is that population health improvement will not be achieved until appropriate financial incentives are designed for this outcome. It calls for Purchasing Population Health, operationalized as units of health adjusted life expectancy, to be the new definitional and incentive paradigm of the early-twenty-first century. It will be new, not in its concept or even its demonstration, but in that it will be built into fundamental financial and organizational structures that transcend fad or ideology. It will begin to reverse the current incentives that reward for increasing investments in medical care without a measure of their effectiveness.

This is not a Don Quixote scheme for the distant future; we are on the verge of outcome measurement and public and private demand for value. This can realistically be achieved over the 25 year period outlined. The fact that it is primarily a technical innovation without dramatic national social and political reform is consistent with U.S. values and approaches and significantly improves the potential for its realization.

Simply put, implementing such an approach to measure and pay for cost-effective improvement in population health status is the best opportunity we have for bringing value to U.S. patients and purchasers as we enter the twenty-first century.

Reference List

Adler, N. E., T. Boyce, M. Chesney, S. Cohen, S. Folkman, R. Kahn, and S. Syme. 1994. Socioeconomic Status and Health: The Challenge of the Gradient. *American Psychologist* 49:15–24.

Adler, N. E., T. Boyce, M. Chesney, S. Folkman, and S. Syme. 1993. Socioeconomic Inequalities in Health: No Easy Solution. *JAMA* 269 (24): 3140–45.

Afifi, A., and L. Breslow. 1994. The Maturing Paradigm of Public Health. *Ann. Rev. Pub. Health* 15:223–35.

Albrecht, G. L., ed. 1994. *Quality of Life in Health Care. Advances in Medical Sociology.* Greenwich: JAI Press.

Altman, S., and M. Ostby. 1991. Paying for Hospital Care: The Impact of Federal Policy. In *Health Services Research: Key to Policy*, ed. E. Ginzberg. Cambridge: Harvard University Press.

American Hospital Association (AHA). 1993. *Transforming Health Care Delivery: Toward Community Care Networks.* Chicago: American Hospital Association.

———. 1995. *The Community Care Network Demonstration.* Chicago: American Hospital Association.

Auster, R., I. Leveson, and D. Sarachek. 1969. The Production of Health: An Exploratory Study. *J. Human Resources* 4:411–36.

Avis, N. E., and K. E. Smith. 1994 Conceptual and Methodological Issues in Selecting and Developing Quality of Life Measures. In *Quality of Life in Health Care. Advances in Medical Sociology*, ed. G. L. Albrecht, 255–80. Greenwich: JAI Press.

Baird, P. A. 1994. The Role of Genetics in Population Health. Chap. 5. in *Why Are Some People Healthy and Others Not? The Determinants of Health of Populations*, ed. R. Evans, M. Barer, and T. Marmor. New York: Aldine de Gruyter.

Barker, D. J. P., and C. Osmond. 1987. Inequalities in Health in Britain. Specific Explanations in Three Lancashire Towns. *Brit. Med. J.* 294:749–52.

Berkman, L. 1984. Assessing the Physical Health Effects of Social Networks and Social Support. *Ann. Rev. Public Health* 5:413–32.

———. 1995. The Role of Social Relations in Health Promotion. *Psychosomatic Medicine* 57:245–54.

Berkman, L., and L. Syme. 1979. Social Networks, Host Resistance, and Mortality. *Am. J. Epidem.* 109 (2): 186–204.

Berwick, D. M. 1988. Toward an Applied Technology for Quality Measurement in Health Care. *Med. Decis. Making* 8:253–58.

———. 1989. Continuous Improvement as an Ideal in Health Care. *N. Engl. J. Med.* 320:53–56.

———. 1994. Eleven Worthy Aims for Clinical Leadership of Health System Reform. *JAMA* 272 (10): 797–802.

Birch, S., and A. Maynard. 1986. Performance Indicators and Performance Assessment in the UK National Health Service. *Int. J. of Health Planning and Management* 1:143–56.

Blumenthal, D. 1996. Quality of Health Care: What Is It? *N. Engl. J. Med.* 335 (12): 891–94.

Bosna, H., M. Marmot, H. Hemingway, A. Nicholson, E. Brunner, and S. Stansfield. 1997. Low Job Control and Risk of Coronary Heart Disease in Whitehall II Study. *Brit. Med. J.* 314: 558–65.

Breslow, L. 1990. The Future of Public Health. Prospects for the United States for the 1990s. *Ann. Rev. Pub. Health* 11:1–28.

Broder, D. S., and H. Johnson. 1996. *The System.* New York: Little, Brown.

Brook, R., C. Kamberg, and E. McGlynn. 1996. Health System Reform and Quality. *JAMA* 276 (6): 476–80.

Brooks, R. G. 1995. Health Status Measurement: A Perspective on Change. Houndmills, England: Macmillan Press.

Brown, P. 1995. Race, Class, and Environmental Health. A Review and Systematization of the Literature. *Environ. Res.* 69:15–30.

Bunker, J. 1995. Medicine Matters after All. *J. Royal Coll. Phys. London* 29 (2): 105–12.

Bunker, J., H. Frazier, and F. Mosteller. 1994. Improving Health: Measuring the Effects of Medical Care. *Milbank Mem. Fund. Quart.* 74 (summer): 225–59.

Burner, S., and D. Waldo. 1995. National Health Expenditure Projections. 1994–2005. *Health Care Financing Review* 16 (4): 221–42.

Cairns, J. 1992. Discounting and Health Benefits: Another Perspective. *Health Econ.* 1:76–79.

Carroll, L. 1984. *Alice's Adventures in Wonderland.* London: Macmillan Children's.

Catholic Hospital Association (CHA). 1992. *Setting Relationships Right: A Proposal for Systemic Healthcare Reform.* St. Louis: Catholic Hospital Association.

———. 1995. *A Handbook for Planning and Developing Integrated Delivery.* Chicago: Catholic Hospital Association.

Centers for Disease Control and Prevention. 1995. Prevention and Managed Care. *Morbidity and Mortality Weekly Report* 44 (November 17, RR–14): 1–12.

Challis, D., and B. Davies. 1986. *Case Management in Community Care.* Aldershot: Gower Press.

Chen, W. K. 1976. A Comprehensive Population Health Index Based on Mortality and Disability Data. *Soc. Indicators Res.* 3:257–71.

———. 1979. The Gross National Health Product: A Proposed Population Health Index. *Pub. Health Rep.* 94:119–23.

Cherkasky, M. 1992. Leadership and Social Responsibility. In *The Role of the Physician Executive,* ed. D. Kindig and A. Kovner. Ann Arbor: Health Administration Press.

Chewning, B. 1993. Evaluating the Computer as a Data Camera in Family Planning Research. *Advances in Population* 1:85–103.

Cleary, P., I. Wilson, and F. Fowler. 1994. A Theoretical Framework for Assessing and Analyzing Health Related Quality of Life. In *Quality of Life in Health Care. Advances in Medical Sociology,* ed. G. L. Albrecht, 23–41. Greenwich: JAI Press.

Conrad, D., and W. Dowling. 1990. Vertical Integration in Health Services: Theory and Managerial Implications. *Health Care Mgt. Rev.* 15 (4): 9–22.

Conrad, D., and S. Shortell. 1996. Integrated Health Systems: Promise and Performance. *Frontiers of Health Services Management* 13 (1): 3–40.

Culyer, A. J. 1988. The Normative Economics of Health Care Finance and Provision. *Oxford Review of Economic Policy* 5 (1): 34–58.

———. 1993. Health, Health Expenditures, and Equity. In *Equity in the Finance and Delivery of Health Care,* ed. E. VanDoorslaer et al. Oxford: Oxford University Press.

———. 1995. Need: The Idea Won't Do, but We Still Need It. *Soc. Sci. Med.* 40 (6): 727–30.

Culyer, A. J., and A. Wagstaff. 1993. Equity and Equality in Health Care. *J. Health Econ.* 12 (4): 431–57.

Daedalus: J. of the Am. Academy of Arts and Sciences. 1994. Special Issue. Health and Wealth. 123 (4) (fall).

Daniels, N. 1985. *Just Health Care.* Cambridge: Cambridge University Press.

———. 1991. Is the Oregon Rationing Plan Fair? *JAMA* 265 (17): 2232–35.

Dar, E., M. Kanarek, M. Anderson, and W. Sonzogni. 1992. Fish Consumption and Reproductive Outcome in Green Bay, Wisc. *Environ. Research* 59:189–201.

Davey Smith, G., M. Bartley, and D. Blane. 1990. The Black Report on Socioeconomic Inequalities in Health 10 Years On. *Brit. Med. J.* 301:373–77.

Davey Smith, G., C. Hart, D. Blane, C. Gilllis, and V. Hawthorne. 1997. Lifetime Socioeconomic Position and Mortality. *Brit. Med. J.* 314:547–52.

Dean, A. G., D. West, and W. Weir. 1982. Measuring Loss of Life, Health and Income Due to Disease and Injury. *Pub. Health Rep.* 97 (1): 38–47.

Delbanco, T. 1996. In Just Say No, by J. Green. *New York Times,* Sunday, September 15, 84.

Deming, W. E. 1986. *Out of the Crisis.* Cambridge: MIT.

Dixon, J., and H. Glennerster. 1995. What Do We Know about Fundholding in General Practice? *Brit. Med. J.* 311:727–30.

Dolan, P., and C. Gudex. 1995. Time Preference, Duration, and Health State Valuations. *Health Econ.* 4:289–99.

Donabedian, A. 1980. *Explorations in Quality Assurance and Monitoring.* Vol. 1, *The Definition of Quality and Approaches to Its Measurement.* Ann Arbor: Health Administration Press.

Donahue, J. D. 1989. *The Privatization Decision: Public Ends, Private Means.* New York: Basic Books.

Dressler, W. 1991. Social Class, Skin Color, and Arterial Blood Pressure in Two Societies. *Ethnicity and Disease* 1:60–77.

Drummond, M., E. Mohide, and M. Tew, et al. 1991. Economic Evaluation of a Support Program for Caregivers of Demented Elderly. *Int. J. of Tech. Assessment in Health Care* 7 (2): 209–19.

Drummond, M., and G. Stoddart. 1995. Assessment of Health Producing Measures across Different Sectors. *Health Policy* 33:219–31.

Drummond, M., G. Stoddart, and G. Torrance. 1987. Methods for Economic Evaluation of Health Programmes. Oxford: Oxford Medical Publications.

Drummond, M., G. Torrance, and J. Mason. 1993. Cost-Effectiveness League Tables: More Harm than Good? *Soc. Sci. Med.* 37 (1): 33–40.

Dubois, R., and R. Brook. 1988. Preventable Deaths: Who, How Often, and Why? *Ann. Int. Med.* 109:582–89.

Eddy, D. M. 1991a. Oregon's Methods: Did Cost-Effectiveness Fail? *JAMA* 266 (15): 2135–41.

———. 1991b. Oregon's Plan; Should It Be Approved? *JAMA* 266 (17): 2439–45.

———. 1994. Rationing Resources while Improving Quality: How to Get More for Less. *JAMA* 272 (18): 817–24.

Ellwood, P. 1988. Outcomes Management: A Technology of Patient Experience. *N. Engl. J. Med.* 318:1549–56.

Ellwood, P., and G. Lundberg. 1996. Managed Care: A Work in Progress. *JAMA* 276 (13): 1083–86.

Epstein, A. 1995. Performance Reports on Quality—Prototypes, Problems, and Prospects. *N. Engl. J Med.* 333 (1): 57–61.

Erickson, P., R. Wilson, and I. Shannon. 1995. *Years of Healthy Life.* NCHS Healthy People Statistical Notes #7. USPHS. April.

Evans, R., M. Barer, and T. Marmor. 1994. *Why Are Some People Healthy and Others Not? The Determinants of Health of Populations.* New York: Aldine de Gruyter.

Evans, R., M. Hodge, and I. Pless. 1994. If Not Genetics, Then What? Biological Pathways and Population Health. Chap. 6 in *Why Are Some People Healthy and Others Not? The Determinants of Health of Populations,* ed. R. Evans, M. Barer, and T. Marmor. New York: Aldine de Gruyter.

Evans, R., and G. Stoddart. 1990. Consuming Health Care, Producing Health. *Soc. Sci. Med.* 31 (12): 1347–63.

Eyles, J., S. Birch, S. Chambers, J. Hurley, and B. Hutchison. 1991. A Needs Based Methodology for Allocating Health Care Resources in Ontario, Canada. *Soc. Sci. Med.* 33 (4): 489–500.

Feagin, J. 1991. The Continuing Significance of Race: Antiblack Discrimination in Public Places. *Am. Sociol. Review* 56:101–16.

Feldman, J. J., D. Makuc, J. Kleinman, and J. Cornoni-Huntley. 1989. National Trends in Educational Differences in Mortality. *Am. J. Epidem.* 129 (5): 919–31.

Fielding, J. 1995. Determinants of Health. Draft presented to the Canadian Institute for Advanced Research Population Health Program, January 15.

Foege, W. 1994. Preventive Medicine and Public Health. *JAMA* 271:1704–5.

Fordham Institute. 1996. *1996 Index of Social Health—Monitoring the Social Well Being of the Nation.* Tarrytown: Fordham Institute for Innovation in Social Policy.

Fowles, J., J. Weiner, D. Knutson, E. Fowler, A. Tucker, and M. Ireland. 1996. Taking Health Status into Account When Setting Capitation Rates. *JAMA* 276 (16): 1316–21.

Fryback, D. 1993. QUALYs, HYEs, and the Loss of Innocence. *Med. Decis. Making* 13 (4): 271–72.

Fryback, D., E. Dasbach, R. Klein, B. Klein, N. Dorn, K. Peterson, and P. Martin. 1993. The Beaver Dam Health Outcomes Study: Initial Catalog of Health State Quality Factors. *Med. Decis. Making* 13 (2): 89–102.

Fuchs, Victor. 1974. *Who Shall Live?* Basic Books, New York.

———. 1983. *How We Live: An Economic Perspective on Americans from Birth to Death.* Cambridge: Harvard University Press.

Fuchs, V., and J. Hahn. 1990. A Comparison of Expenditures for Physicians Services in the United States and Canada. *New. Engl. J. Med.* 323:884–90.

Giacomini, M., H. Luft, and J. Robinson. 1995. Risk Adjusting Community Rated Health Premiums. *Ann. Rev. Pub. Health* 16:401–30.

Gold, M., J. Siegel, L. Russell, and M. C. Weinstein. 1996. *Cost Effectiveness in Health and Medicine.* New York: Oxford University Press.

Goldsmith, J. 1994. The Illusive Logic of Integration. *Healthcare Forum J.,* September–October, 26–31.

———. 1995. Managed Care Comes of Age. *Healthcare Forum J.,* September–October, 14–24.

Gornick, M., P. Eggers, T. Reilley, R. Mentnech, L. Fitterman, L. Kucken, and B. Vladeck. 1996. Effects of Race and Income on Mortality and Use of Services among Medicare Beneficiaries. *N. Engl. J. Med.* 335 (11): 791–98.

Gosfield, A. 1997. Who Is Holding Whom Accountable for Quality. *Health Affairs* 16 (3): 26–39.

Grosse, R., and C. Auffrey. 1989. Literacy and Health Status in Developing Countries. *Ann. Rev. Pub. Health* 10:281–97.

Grossman, M. 1972. *Demand for Health.* New York: National Bureau of Economic Research.

Gruenberg, E. M. 1977. The Failure of Success. *Milbank Mem. Fund Quart.* 55:3–24.

Guralnik, J., K. Land, and D. Blazer. 1993. Educational Status and Active Life Expectancy among Older Blacks and Whites. *N. Engl. J. Med.* 329 (2): 110–16.

Gustafson, D., C. Bosworth, B. Chewning, and R. Hawkins. 1987. Computer-Based Health Promotion: Combining Technological Advances with Problem-Solving Techniques to Effect Successful Health Behavior Changes. *Ann. Rev. Public Health* 8:387–415.

Hadley, J. 1982. *More Medical Care, Better Health?* Washington, DC: Urban Institute Press.

Hadorn, D. 1991. Setting Health Care Priorities in Oregon: Cost Effectiveness Meets the Rule of Rescue. *JAMA* 265 (17): 2218–25.

Harrigan, K. 1984. Formulating Vertical Integration Strategies. *Acad. Mgt. Rev.* 9 (4): 638–52.

Harrington, C., R. Newcomer, and S. Preston. 1993. A Comparison of SHMO Disenrollees and Continuing Members. *Inquiry* 30:429–40.

Harris, J. 1987. QALYfying the Value of Life. *J. Med. Ethics* 13 (3): 117–23.

———. 1988. More and Better Justice. In *Philosophy and Medical Welfare,* ed. J. Bell and S. Mendus, 79–96. Cambridge: Cambridge University Press.

Health Care Financing Administration (HCFA). 1996. Medicare Beneficiary Health Status Registry and Beneficiary Centered Purchasing. Health Care Financing Administration Draft Communications.

Healthcare Forum Journal. 1997. Healthy Community Projects. May/June, 37–49.

HEDIS/Report Cards. 1997. Hedis 3.0 Executive Summary. Www.ncqa.org/hedis/30exsum.htm, March.

Henderson, H. 1991. *Paradigms in Progress: Life beyond Economics.* Indianapolis: Knowledge Systems.

Hertzman, C. 1994. The Lifelong Impact of Childhood Experiences: A Population Health Perspective. *Daedalus: J. of the Am. Academy of Arts and Sciences,* Special Issue, Health and Wealth, 123 (4) (fall): 167–80.

Hertzman, C., J. Frank, and R. Evans. 1994. Heterogeneities in Health Status. Chap. 3 in *Why Are Some People Healthy and Others Not? The Determinants of Health of Populations,* ed. R. Evans, M. Barer, and T. Marmor. New York: Aldine de Gruyter.

House, J. S., K. Landis, and D. Umberson. 1988. Social Relationships and Health. *Science* 241:540–45.

Hummer, R. A. 1996. Black-White Differences in Health and Mortality. *Soc. Quart.* 37 (1): 105–25.

Iezzoni, L. 1994. *Risk Adjustment for Measuring Health Care Outcome.* Ann Arbor: Health Administration Press.

Iglehart, J. 1996. The National Committee for Quality Assurance. *N. Engl. J. Med.* 335 (13): 995–99.

Illich, I. 1976. *Medical Nemesis: The Expropriation of Health.* New York: Pantheon Books.

Institute of Medicine. 1988. *The Future of Public Health.* Washington, DC: National Academy Press.

Isham, G. 1997. Personal communication regarding Health Partners, Minneapolis.

Jencks, S. 1995. Measuring Quality of Care under Medicare and Medicaid. *Health Care Financing Review* 16:39–54.

Johnson, H. 1995. *Green Plans: Greenprint for Sustainability.* Lincoln: University of Nebraska Press.

Johnston, R., and P. Lawrence. 1988. Beyond Vertical Integration: The Rise of the Value Added Partnership. *Harvard Business Review* (July–August): 94–100.

Judge, K. 1995. Income Distribution and Life Expectancy: A Critical Appraisal. *Brit. Med. J.* 311:1282–85.

Kaplan, G., E. Pamuk, J. Lynch, R. Cohen, and J. Balfour. 1996. Inequality in Income and Mortality in the United States: An Analysis of Mortality and Potential Pathways. *Brit. Med. J.* 312:999–1003.

Kassirer, J. 1993. The Quality of Health Care and the Quality of Measuring It. *N. Engl. J. Med.* 329:1263–65.

Katz, S., L. Branch, and M. Branson. 1983. Active Life Expectancy. *N. Engl. J. Med.* 309:1218–24.

Kehrer, B. H., and C. M. Wolin. 1979. Impact of Income Maintenance on Low Birth Weight: Evidence from the Gary Experiment. *J. Human Resources* 14 (4): 434–62.

Kettl, D. 1994. Deregulating the Boundaries of Government: Would It Help? In *Deregulating the Public Service,* ed. J. Diulio. Washington, DC: Brookings.

Kickbush, I. 1994. Ecological Public Health—The Department of Consequences. Health Care Forum Draft, May.

Kind, P., C. Gudex, and P. Dolan. 1994. Practical and Methodological Experience with the Development of the EuroQuol. In *Quality of Life in Health Care: Advances in Medical Sociology,* ed. G. L. Albrecht, 219–53. Greenwich: JAI Press.

Kindig, D. 1993. The Health Care System Should Produce Health. *Phys. Executive* 19 (4): 79–80.

Kindig, D., and D. Libby. 1994. Setting State Health Spending Targets. *Health Affairs* spring (second issue): 288–89.

King, M., G. Lee, N. Spinner, G. Thompson, and M. Wrensch. 1984. Genetic Epidemiology. *Ann. Rev. Pub. Health* 5:1–52.

Kitagawa, E., and P. Hauser. 1973. *Differential Mortality in the United States: A Study in Socioeconomic Epidemiology.* Cambridge: Harvard University Press.

Kleinman, J., and J. H. Madans. 1985. Effects of Maternal Smoking, Physical Stature, and Educational Attainment on the Incidence of Low Birth Weight. *Am. J. Epidem.* 121 (6): 843–55.

Knowles, J. *Doing Better and Feeling Worse: Health in the United States.* New York: Norton.

Koren, H. 1995. *Handbook of Environmental Health and Safety.* Boca Raton: Lewis Publishers.

Lansky, D. 1996. The Facts about FACCT. *Accountability Action* 1 (1): 5–8.

Leape, L. 1994. Error in Medicine. *JAMA* 272:1851–57.

Lee, P. 1995. Speech at the University of Wisconsin School of Medicine, October.

Lee, P., and D. Paxman. 1997. Reinventing Public Health. *Ann. Rev. Public Health* 18:1–35.

Levit, K., H. Lazenby, B. Braden, C. Cowan, P. McDonnell, L. Sivarajan, J. Stiller, D. Won, C. Donham, A. Long, and M. Stewart. 1996. National Health Expenditures 1995. *Health Care Financing Review* 18 (1): 175–214.

Levit, K., H. Lazenby, C. Cowan, D. Won, J. Stiller, L. Sivarajan, and M. Stewart. 1995. State Health Expenditure Accounts: Building Blocks for State Health Spending Analysis. *Health Care Financing Review* 17 (1): 201–54.

Lewin Group. 1996. Recent Trends in Employer Health Insurance Coverage and Benefits. Prepared for the American Hospital Association, Sept. 3, 1996.

Libby, D., and D. Kindig. 1996. State Health Status and Health Expenditure. Working paper, University of Wisconsin Network for Health Policy Research.

Lillienfield, D. E., and P. D. Stolley. 1994. *Foundations of Epidemiology.* 3d ed. New York: Oxford University Press.

Linder, F. E. 1996. The Health of the American People. *Scientific American* 214 (6): 21–29.

Lipset, S. M. 1966. *American Exceptionalism: A Double-Edged Sword.* New York: Norton.

Lohr, K. 1990. *Medicare: A Strategy for Quality Assurance.* Washington, DC: Institute of Medicine, National Academy Press.

———. 1992. Advances in Health Status. *Medical Care* 30 (5) (May) Supplement.

Lockwood, M. 1988. Quality of Life and Resource Allocation. In *Philosophy and Medical Welfare,* ed. J. Bell and S. Mendus, 33–55. Cambridge: Cambridge University Press.

Lomas, J., M. Rachlis, and S. Kumar. 1996. *Block Funding for Human Services in Prince Edward Island: A Case Study of an Incentive for Cross Sectoral Reallocations.* Final report to Health Canada, March 1996.

Lomas, J., J. Woods, and G. Veenstra. 1996. Devolving Authority for Health in Canada's Provinces. Working paper, McMasters University.

Luft, H. 1996. Modifying Managed Competition to Address Cost and Quality. *Health Affairs* 15 (spring): 23–38.

Luft, H., and E. Morrison. 1991. Alternate Delivery Systems. In *Health Services Research: Key to Health Policy,* ed. E. Ginzberg. Cambridge: Harvard University Press.

Maddox, G. L., and E. B. Douglass. 1973. Self-Assessment of Health: A Longitudinal Study of Elderly Patients. *J. Health Soc. Behav.* 14:87–93.

Maibach, E., and D. R. Holtgrave. 1995. Advances in Public Health Communication. *Ann. Rev. Pub. Health* 16:2219–38.

Manton, K. G. 1982. Changing Concepts of Morbidity and Mortality in the Elderly Population. *Milbank Mem. Fund Quart.* 60:183–244.

Manton, K. G., L. Corder, and E. Stallard. 1995. Changes in Morbidity and Chronic Disability in the U.S. Elderly Population: Evidence from the 1982, 1984, and 1989 National Long Term Care Surveys. *J. Gerontol.* 50B (4): 5195–204.

———. 1997. Chronic Disability Trends in Elderly United States Populations: 1982–1994. *Proc. Natl. Acad. Sci.* 94:2593–98.

Manuck, S., J. Kaplan, and K. Matthews. 1986. Behavioral Antecedents of Coronary Artery Disease and Atherosclerosis. *Atherosclerosis* 6:2–14.

Marmot, M. 1994. Social Differentials in Health within and between Populations. *Daedalus: J. of the Am. Academy of Arts and Sciences*, Special Issue, Health and Wealth, 123 (4) (fall): 197–216.

Marmot, M., and G. Davey-Smith. 1989. Why Are the Japanese Living Longer? *Brit. Med. J.* 299:1547–51.

Marmot, M., M. Kogevinas, and M. Elston. 1987. Social Economic Status and Disease. *Ann. Rev. Pub. Health* 8:111–35.

Marmot, M., G. Rose, M. J. Shipley, and P. H. S. Hamilton. 1978. Employment Grade and Coronary Heart Disease in British Civil Servants. *J. Epidem. and Comm. Health.* 32:244–49.

Marmot, M., and T. Theorell. 1988. Social Class and Cardiovascular Disease: The Contribution of Work. *Int. J. Health Serv.* 18:659–74.

Maynard, A. 1995. Ethical Issues in the Economics of Rationing Healthcare. *Brit. J. Urology* 76:59–64.

Mays, N., and J. Dixon. 1996. *Purchaser Plurality in UK Health Care.* London: Kings Fund.

McGinnis, M., and W. H. Foege. 1993. Actual Causes of Death in the United States. *JAMA* 270 (18): 2207–12.

McGinnis, M., and P. Lee. 1995. Healthy People 2000 at Mid Decade. *JAMA* 273 (14): 1123–29.

McHorney, C. 1994. Methodologic Issues in Health Status Assessment across Populations and Applications. In *Quality of Life in Health Care. Advances in Medical Sociology,* ed. G. L. Albrecht, 281–304. Greenwich: JAI Press.

———. 1996. Measuring Health Status in the Elderly with the SF-36 Health Survey: Practical and Methodological Issues. *Gerontologist* 36 (5): 571–83.

McKeown, T. 1976. *The Role of Medicine: Dream, Mirage or Nemesis?* London: Nuffield Provincial Hospital Trust.

McKinlay, J. B., S. McKinlay, and R. Beaglehole. 1989. Review of the Evidence concerning the Impact of Medical Measures on the Recent Morbidity and Mortality in the United States. *Int. J. Health Services* 19 (2): 181–208.

Miller, R., and H. Luft. 1995. Estimating Health Expenditure Growth under Managed Competition. *JAMA* 273:656–62.

Merget, A. 1994. Behind the Scenes: The Doing of Public Administration. Speech at the National Association of Schools of Public Affairs, Tucson, October.

Moeller, D. 1992. *Environmental Health.* Cambridge: Harvard University Press.

Morton, N. E. 1993. Genetic Epidemiology. *Ann. Rev. Genetics* 27:523–38.

Mossey, J. A., and E. Shapiro. 1982. Self-Rated Health: A Predictor of Mortality among the Elderly. *Am. J. Pub. Health* 72 (8): 800–808.

Mullahy, J., and P. Portney. 1990. Air Pollution, Cigarette Smoking, and the Protection of Respiratory Health. *J. Health. Econ.* 9 (2): 193–206.

Murray, C. J. L. 1994. Quantifying the Burden of Disease: The Technical Basis for Disability-Adjusted Life Years. *Bull. World Health Org.* 72:429–45.

New York Times. 1996. Editorial, The New Clinton Health Panel, September 11, sec. 1.

New York Times. 1997. Health Care Costs Edging up, and a Bigger Surge Is Feared, January 21, sec. 1.

Nightingale, F. 1863. *Notes on Hospitals.* London: Longmans, Green, and Company; reprinted in C. Rosenberg, ed. 1989. *Florence Nightingale on Hospital Reform.* New York and London: Garland Publishing.

Nord, E. 1994. The QALY—A Measure of Social Value Rather than Individual Utility? *Health Econ.* 3:89–93.

Northwestern National Life Insurance Company. 1993. *The NWNL State Health Rankings.* 1993 ed. Minneapolis: Northwestern National Life Insurance Company.

Office of Technology Assessment, U.S. Congress. 1992. *Evaluation of the Oregon Medicaid Proposal.* OTA-H-531. Washington, DC.

Olsen, J. A. 1994. Persons vs. Years: Two Ways of Eliciting Implicit Weights. *Health Econ.* 3:39–46.

O'Neill, M. 1996. Helping School Children with Asthma Breathe Easier. *Environ. Health Perspect.* 104 (5): 464–66.

Ostro, B. 1983. The Effects of Air Pollution on Work Loss and Morbidity. *J. Environ. Econ. and Mgt.* 10:371–82.

Palmer, H. 1995. Securing Health Care Quality for Medicine. *Health Affairs* 14 (4): 89–100.

Pappas, G., S. Queens, M. Hadden, and G. Fisher. 1993. The Increasing Disparity in Mortality between Socioeconomic Groups in the United States, 1960 and 1964. *N. Engl. J. Med.* 329 (2): 103–9.

Patrick, D., and M. Bergner. 1990. The Measurement of Health Status in the 1990s. *Ann. Rev. Pub. Health* 11:165–83.

Patrick, D., and R. A. Deyo. 1989. Generic and Disease Specific Measures in Assessing Health Status and Quality of Life. *Med. Care* 27 (3): S217–32.

Patrick, D., and P. Erickson. 1993. Health Status and Health Policy: Allocating Resources to Health Care. New York: Oxford University Press.

Phelps, C. 1997. Good Technologies Gone Bad: How and Why the Cost-Effectiveness of a Medical Intervention Changes for Different Populations. *Med. Decis. Making* 17 (1): 107–17.

Pickle, W., M. Mungiole, G. Jones, and A. White. 1997. *Atlas of United States Mortality.* Hyattsville, MD: National Center for Health Statistics.

Platts-Mills, T., and M. Carter. 1997. Asthma and Indoor Exposure to Allergens. *N. Engl. J. Med.* 336:1382–84.

Porter, M. 1985. *Comparative Advantage.* New York: Free Press.

Putnam, R. D. 1993. The Prosperous Community: Social Capital and Public Life. *American Prospect* 13 (spring): 35–42.

Quebec Ministry of Health. 1989. *Orientations: Improving Health and Well Being in Quebec.*

Rawls, J. 1971. *A Theory of Justice.* Cambridge: Harvard University Press.

Reichlin, S. 1993. Neuroendocrine-Immune Interactions. *N. Engl. J. Med.* 329 (17): 1246–53.

Reinhardt, U. 1996. Rationing Health Care. In *Strategic Choices for a Changing Health Care System,* ed. S. Altman and U. Reinhardt. Chicago: Health Administration Press.

Reiser, S. 1996. Medicine and Public Health: Pursuing a Common Destiny. *JAMA* 276 (17): 1429–30.

Reynolds, R. 1976. Improving Access to Health Care among the Poor—The Neighborhood Health Center Experience. *Milbank Mem. Fund Quart.* 54 (1): 47–82.

Richardson, E. 1996. *Reflections of a Radical Moderate.* New York: Pantheon.

Riley, T. 1997. The Role of States in Accountability for Quality. *Health Affairs* 16 (3): 41–43.

Rivlin, A., and J. Woiner. 1988. Social Health Maintenance Organizations. In *Caring for the Disabled Elderly: Who Will Pay?* Washington, DC: Brookings Press.

Robine, J. M. 1993. Distinguishing Health Expectancies and Health Adjusted Life Expectancies from Quality Adjusted Life Years. *Am. J. Pub. Health* 83 (6): 797–98.

Robine, J. M., and K. Ritchie. 1991. Healthy Life Expectancy: Evaluation of Global Indicator of Change in Population Health. *Brit. Med. J.* 302:457–60.

Roos, N., C. Black, N. Frohlich, and C. DeCoster. 1996. Population Health and Health Care Use: An Information System for Health Policy Makers. *Milbank Mem. Fund Quart.* 74 (1): 3–29.

Roos, N., and E. Shapiro. 1995. Health and Health Care: Experience with a Population-Based Health Information System. *Medical Care* 33 (12) (December) Supplement.

Rosser, R. M., and P. Kind. 1978. A Scale of Valuations of States of Illness: Is There a Social Consensus? *Int. J. of Epidem.* 7:347–58.

Rowland, D., and K. Hanson. 1996. Medicaid: Moving to Managed Care. *Health Affairs* 15 (31): 150–52.

Rundall, T. 1994. Closing the Loop: The Integration of Public Health and Personal Health Services. *Frontiers of Health Services Management* 10 (4): 3–24.

Ryan, M. 1996. *Using Conjoint Analysis to Go beyond Health Outcomes: An Application to In Vitro Fertilization.* Vancouver: International Health Economics Association, May 20.

Sapolsky, R. 1990. Stress in the Wild. *Scientific American* 262 (1): 116–23.

Scott, R. 1996. Taming a Hydra Headed Health Policy, Columbia/HCA "Policy Forum." *Newsweek,* November 11.

Sen, A. 1992. *On Ethics and Economics.* Oxford: Blackwell Press.

Sheldon, T. 1992. Discounting in Health Care Decision Making . . . Time for a Change? *J. Pub. Health Med.* 14 (3): 250–56.

Shortell, S. 1992. A Model for State Health Reform. *Health Affairs* 11 (spring): 108–27.

Shortell, S., R. Gilles, D. Anderson, K. Erickson, and J. Mitchell. 1996. Remaking Health Care in America: Building Organized Delivery Systems. San Francisco: Jossey-Bass.

Shortell, S., and K. Hull. 1996. The New Organization of the Health Care Delivery System. In *Strategic Choices for a Changing Health Care System,* ed. S. Altman and U. Reinhardt. Chicago: Health Administration Press.

Sigmond, R. 1995. Collaboration in a Competitive Environment: The Pursuit of Community Health. *Frontiers of Health Services Management* 11 (4): 5–36.

Singer, P., J. McKie, H. Kuhse, and J. Richardson. 1995. Double Jeopardy and the Use of QALYs in Health Care Allocation. *J. Med. Ethics* 21:144–50.

Smith, G. D. et al. 1990. The Black Report on Socioeconomic Inequalities in Health 10 Years On. *Brit. Med. J.* 301:373–77.

Smith, P. 1995. On the Unintended Consequences of Publishing Performance Data in the Public Sector. *Int. J. of Public Admin.* 18:277–310.

Smith, R. 1996. Rationing Health Care: Moving the Debate Forward. *Brit. Med. J.* 312:1553–54.

Snowdon, D., S. Kemper, J. Mortimer, L. Greiner, D. Wekstein, and W. Markesbery. 1996. Linguistic Ability in Early Life and Cognitive Function and Alzheimer's Disease in Later Life. *JAMA* 275 (17): 528–32.

Sommer, A. 1995. Whither Public Health? *Pub. Health Rep.* 110:657–61.

Steinbrook, R. 1997. Allocating Livers—Devising a Fair System. *N. Engl. J. Med.* 336 (6): 436–38.

Sullivan, D. F. 1971. A Single Index of Mortality and Morbidity. *HSMHA Reports* 86:347–54.

Swedish Ministry of Health and Social Affairs. 1995. Press release, December 14.

Tarlov, A. 1996. *National Standards for Health Plans Now Include Outcomes.* Medical Outcomes Trust Bulletin, September. Boston: Medical Outcomes Trust.

Tarlov, A., J. Ware, S. Greenfield, R. Nelson, E. Perrin, and M. Zubkoff. 1989. The Medical Outcomes Study: An Application of the Methods for Monitoring the Results of Medical Care. *JAMA* 262:925–30.

Tengs, T., M. Adams, J. Pliskin, D. Safran, J. H. Siegel, M. Weinstein, and J. Graham. 1995. Five Hundred Life-Saving Interventions and Their Cost Effectiveness. *Risk Analysis* 15 (3): 369–90.

Toomey, K., and P. Lee. 1994. Epidemiology in Public Health in the Era of Health Care Reform. *Public Health Reports* 109 (January/February): 1–3.

Torrance, G. W. 1986. Measurement of Health State Utilities for Economic Appraisal. *J. Health Econ.* 5:1–30.

USA Today. 1996. Despite Complaints, New Transplant Priorities Better, November 22.

———. 1997. Businesses Leery of Health Care Quality, March 14.

U.S. Department of Health and Human Services (USDHHS). 1991. *Healthy People 2000: National Health Promotion and Disease Prevention Objectives.* PHS 91-50212. Washington, DC.

————. 1996. *Health United States 1995.* DHHS Publication 96-1232. Hyattsville. May.

U.S. General Accounting Office. 1995. *Block Grants: Characteristics, Experience, and Lessons Learned.* GAO/HEHS-95-74. Washington, DC. November.

————. 1996. *Public Health: A Health Status Indicator for Targeting Federal Aid to States.* GAO/HEHS-97-13. November.

Vagero, D., and D. Lundberg. 1989. Health Inequalities in Britain and Sweden. *Lancet* July 1, 35–36.

Verbrugge, L. M. 1984. Longer Life but Worsening Health? *Milbank Mem. Fund Quart.* 62:475–519.

————. 1989. Recent, Present, and Future Health of American Adults. *Ann. Rev. Pub. Health* 10:333–61.

Waidman, T., J. Bound, and M. Schoenbaum. 1995. The Illusion of Failure: Trends in Self Reported Health of the U.S. Elderly. *Milbank Mem. Fund Quart.* 73 (2): 253–85.

Ware, J. 1995. The Status of Health Assessment 1994. *Ann. Rev. Pub. Health* 16:327–54.

Webster's Third New World International Dictionary. 1976. Springfield, MA: C. Merriam.

Weinberger, M., J. Darnell, W. Tierny, B. Martz, S. Hiner, J. Barker, and P. Neill. 1986. Self-Rated Health as a Predictor of Hospital Admission and Nursing Home Placement in Elderly Public Housing Tenants. *Am. J. Pub. Health* 76 (4): 457–59.

Weinstein, M., J. Siegel, M. Gold, M. Kamlet, and L. Russell. 1996. Recommendations of the Panel on Cost Effectiveness Analysis in Health and Medicine. *JAMA* 276 (15): 1253–58.

Weinstein, M., and W. Stason. 1977. Foundations of Cost-Effectiveness Analysis for Health and Medical Practices. *N. Engl. J. Med.* 296 (13): 716–21.

Welch, W. 1996. Growth in HMO Share of the Medicare Market, 1989–1994. *Health Affairs* 15 (3): 201–14.

Wennberg, J., and A. Gittelsohn. 1982. Variations in Medical Care among Small Areas. *Scientific American* 246:120–35.

Wikler, D. 1992. Persuasion and Coercion for Health. In *Understanding Universal Health Programs,* ed. D. Kindig and R. Sullivan, 88–98. Ann Arbor: Health Administration Press. Quoting Craig Claiborne, In Defense of Eating Rich Food, *New York Times,* December 8, 1976.

Wilkinson, R. G. 1992a. National Mortality Rates: The Impact of Inequality? *Am. J. Pub. Health* 82 (8): 134–36.

————. 1992b. Income Distribution and Life Expectancy. *Brit. Med. J.* 304:165–68.

————. 1994. From Material Scarcity to Social Disadvantage. In *Daedalus: J. of the Am. Academy of Arts and Sciences,* Special Issue, Health and Wealth, 123 (4) (fall): 61–78.

————. 1995. A Reply to Ken Judge: Mistaken Criticisms Ignore Overwhelming Evidence. *Brit. Med. J.* 311:1285–87.

Williams, A. 1974. "Need" as a Demand Concept (with Special Reference to Health). In *Economic Policies and Social Goals,* ed. A. Culyer. London: Martin Robertson.

———. 1986. Economics of Coronary Artery Bypass Grafting. *Brit. Med. J.* 291:326–29.

———. 1988. Ethics and Efficiency in the Provision of Health Care. In *Philosophy and Medical Welfare,* ed. J. Bell and S. Mendus, 111–26. Cambridge: Cambridge University Press.

———. 1992. Cost-Effectiveness Analysis: Is It Ethical? *J. Med. Ethics* 18:7–11.

———. 1996. QALYs and Ethics: A Health Economist's Perspective. *Soc. Sci. Med.*

———. 1997. Rationing Health Care by Age. *Brit. Med. J.* 314:820–22.

Wilson, R. W., and T. F. Drury. 1984. Interpreting Trends in Illness and Disability: Health Statistics and Health Status. *Ann. Rev. Pub. Health* 5:83–106.

Wisconsin State Journal. 1997. State Seeks to Consolidate Services for Elderly, Disabled, May 7.

Wistow, G. 1982. Collaboration between Health and Local Authorities: Is It Necessary? *Soc. Policy and Admin.* 16 (1): 44–62.

———. 1995a. Paying for Long-Term Care: The Shifting Boundary between Health and Social Care. *Community Care Management and Planning* 3 (3): 81–88.

———. 1995b. Aspirations and Realities: Community Care at the Crossroads. *Health and Social Care* 3 (4): 227–40.

Wistow, G., M. Knapp, B. Hardy, and C. Allen. 1995. *Social Care in a Mixed Economy.* Buckingham: Open University Press.

Wolfe, B. 1986. Health Status and Medical Expenditures: Is There a Link? *Soc. Sci. Med.* 22 (10): 993–99.

Wolfson, M. 1994. Social Proprioception: Measurement, Data, and Information from a Population Health Perspective. Chap. 11 in *Why Are Some People Healthy and Others Not? The Determinants of Health of Population,* ed. R. Evans, M. Barer, and T. Marmor. New York: Aldine de Gruyter.

World Bank. 1993. *World Development Report 1993: Investing in Health,* 25–28. New York: Oxford University Press.

World Health Organization. 1978. Alma Ata Declaration, USSR.

Youens, W. 1996. *Prince Edward Islands Health Promotion Framework Learning Guide.* Charlottetown: PEI Community Services Agency.

Zweifel, P., and F. Breyer. 1997. *Health Economics,* chap. 4. New York: Oxford University Press.

Index